Sustainable Ecotourism in Central America

Sustainable Ecotourism in Central America

Comparative Advantage in a Globalized World

Andrew P. Miller

LEXINGTON BOOKS
Lanham • Boulder • New York • London

Published by Lexington Books
An imprint of The Rowman & Littlefield Publishing Group, Inc.
4501 Forbes Boulevard, Suite 200, Lanham, Maryland 20706
www.rowman.com

Unit A, Whitacre Mews, 26-34 Stannary Street, London SE11 4AB

British Library Cataloguing in Publication Information Available

Library of Congress Cataloging-in-Publication Data

Names: Miller, Andrew P., 1961- author.
Title: Sustainable ecotourism in Central America : comparative advantage in a globalized world / Andrew P. Miller.
Description: Lanham : Lexington Books, [2016] | Includes bibliographical references and index.
Identifiers: LCCN 2016031307 (print) | LCCN 2016033376 (ebook) | ISBN 9780739180242 (cloth : alk. paper) | ISBN 9780739180259 (electronic)
Subjects: LCSH: Ecotourism--Costa Rica. | Sustainable tourism--Costa Rica. | Sustainable development--Costa Rica.
Classification: LCC G156.5.E26 M54 2016 (print) | LCC G156.5.E26 (ebook) | DDC 338.4/7917286--dc23
LC record available at https://lccn.loc.gov/2016031307

∞™ The paper used in this publication meets the minimum requirements of American National Standard for Information Sciences Permanence of Paper for Printed Library Materials, ANSI/NISO Z39.48-1992.

Printed in the United States of America

For Christy

Contents

Acknowledgments

The process of writing this book had its ups and downs and would not have been possible without the support of many people along the way. I would first like to thank my colleagues and students at Wilkes University for their support. They listened and commented on nearly every idea in this book. I am very fortunate to teach in a supportive environment with the best colleagues and students a person could want. I would especially like to thank the various student groups that have traveled with me to Costa Rica, Nicaragua, and the Dominican Republic over the years. Thanks also to all of my friends on "The Boulevard," whose friendship is seemingly limitless; nobody has better friends than I. Most of all I would like to thank my wife Christy, nothing I do would be possible without her love and support, this book is dedicated to her.

Introduction

Neoliberalism, Globalization, and the Growth of Sustainable Ecotourism

This introduction lays out the primary thesis of the book, that globalization and neoliberalism have made it more likely that states are able to implement a policy of ecotourism development along with direct foreign investment in order to attract more foreign exchange. Particularly important is the interaction between globalization, neoliberalism, and sustainable ecotourism and the effect of each on economic policy. This introduction also discusses the problems inherent in trying to define ecotourism and suggests that for ecotourism to successfully fulfill its promise it is necessary for states to make policy that explicitly encourages the ecotourism industry to engage in sustainable practices. In many ways, ecotourism is at an important crossroads and one of the best ways to ensure that ecotourism businesses are living up to their promise and doing so in a sustainable way is via ecotourism certification programs. As Fennell and Weaver (2005) argue,

> Contemporary ecotourism is facing a crisis of credibility as a result of two factors. First, numerous tourism products that do not fulfill the widely recognized core criteria of ecotourism are deliberately or inadvertently marketed as such, thereby discrediting those products that do more or less follow the core criteria. Second, it can be argued that most of these legitimate ecotourism products adhere to a weak or minimalist model that impedes or possibly even works against the potential of this sector to serve as a vehicle for environmental, sociocultural and economic sustainability. (373)

For decades, states, at the behest of international organizations, turned to tourism as a steady source of development income. In the face of negative terms of trade, many small economies throughout Latin America and the Caribbean perceived of tourism development as one of their only options and invested large portions of their national budget into developing tourism options. Tourism development was particularly attractive to states based on their ability to deliver traditional sun-and-sand, resort-style tourism due to the tropical environment. Oftentimes this sort of development was accompanied by large-scale foreign investment in which most profits went back to the developed world. For many poor states, the development of tourism represents yet another attempt to find a strategy that would help them to develop economically and toward a better future. For instance, writing about the Republic of the Maldives, Dumroes (2001) states that "[tourism] represents a rational response to the weak economic possibilities on the islands." (134) In this way it is important to understand tourism development as a strategy employed after many other strategies have failed. States throughout the developing world have found it very difficult to develop their economies via agricultural exports and have sought to diversify their exports in order to lower the risk of external shocks. One of the best ways to do this is for a country to diversify its export portfolio with nontraditional exports, including ecotourism. In addition, many of the policy improvements available to states that improve their ability to attract tourists also improve their ability to attract foreign direct investment.

ECOTOURISM IN DISPUTE

For many scholars and businesses, ecotourism is a new type of tourism that provides income for the local population while also preserving the natural environment. From the perspective of the ecotourist, ecotourism provides a way for them to observe fragile flora and fauna while contributing to its preservation should they decide to return in subsequent years. This relationship between the income that can be generated by ecotourism in the present and the need to preserve the natural environment so that income can be generated in the future is the key to understanding the potential of ecotourism development as well as some of its pitfalls. For many, this tension between economic gain and environmental protection is at the heart of the debate over ecotourism and its efficacy as a development tool.

For others, ecotourism is simply seen as a marketing ploy that allows businesses to exploit the environmental consciousness of its customers, while providing very little in the way of sustainable practices. Russell and Wallace (2004) argue that "in its rise to prominence the term 'ecotourism' itself has become so despoiled by unscrupulous operators and a gullible public, that its validity as a concept should be questioned." (1) A great deal of ecotourism literature has centered on the idea that an ecologically-sensitive and sustainable form of tourism is essentially impossible. This book will argue that despite some of its shortcomings, ecotourism provides a tremendous opportunity for economic development in states that have long sought avenues toward a better future. Many of these countries have tried a litany of development strategies, practically all of which have failed. As such, it is important not to think of ecotourism as some sort of panacea, but instead to see it as a new direction in economic development that ties economic growth together with environmental sustainability. Particularly important are policy strategies that link the development of ecotourism to policies that also encourage foreign direct investment as often the pursuit of ecotourism and foreign investment are complementary. In addition, as the world becomes ever smaller due to globalization and the opening of markets based on the ideas of neoliberalism, it is important to assess the impact of each on ecotourism development and the ways in which ecotourism, globalization, and neoliberalism interact with one another.

Part of the problem in defining ecotourism is the myriad definitions and approaches taken by the ecotourism industry and scholars alike. The ecotourism industry has often tended to expand the definition of ecotourism for marketing purposes so that practically anything can be packaged as "ecotourism" including things such as excursions to turtle nesting areas from large cruise ships and ATV tours of the rainforest. For their part, scholars have often extended the definition of ecotourism into ever smaller sub-subfields such as pro-poor tourism, green tourism, and cultural tourism in an attempt to specialize and differentiate into new areas of research. For the most part however, ecotourism (or most of its variants) all return to the same set of overarching principles. For instance, Björk (2000) found more than a dozen ecotourism definitions in wide use in the literature and despite some variance, found that definitions of ecotourism focus on four primary dimensions: the characteristics of the area visited, what the tourists do while visiting, what resources the tourists are interested in, and the effects of the tourist's behavior. (190–91) Despite the difficulties in defining ecotourism since its emergence as a unique tourism form in the 1980s, there are strategies that can be used to help ensure that ecotourism lives up to its promise of providing income for local populations while also maintaining a high standard of sustainability. This is particularly important given that many poor countries rely on ecotourism as a much needed source of foreign exchange.

The debate over the effectiveness of ecotourism as a development strategy has also tended to occur at the extremes with detractors arguing that it is a destructive force that creates little income for anyone except wealthy elites in the United States and Europe and celebrants who argue that ecotourism is the solution to nearly every economic problem in the developing world. In general, the detractors have come from academia and the celebrants have come from the ecotourism industry and international development agencies, which have embraced ecotourism due to its environmentally conscious aspects. While the embrace of ecotourism by international development agencies is relatively new, organizations such as the World Bank and International Monetary Fund have long advocated for states to develop their traditional sun-and-sand tourism industry. In fact, both the United Nations and the World Tourism Organization dubbed 2002 the "International Year of Ecotourism" and developed six main themes for improving the performance of ecotourism around the world: national policy, activities and publications, stakeholder's participation and support, awareness, regulation, and cooperation.

Despite some of the controversies surrounding a precise meaning of ecotourism, the two most widely used definitions are from the International Ecotourism Society, which defines ecotourism as "responsible travel to natural areas that conserves the environment and improves the well-being of local people" (International Ecotourism Society 2014), and from Martha Honey (2008), who in her book *Ecotourism and Sustainable Development: Who Owns Paradise?* develops what has become the most widely used definition of ecotourism which includes these seven parameters:

1. Involves travel to natural destinations.
2. Minimizes impact.
3. Builds environmental awareness.
4. Provides direct financial benefits for conservation.
5. Provides financial benefits and empowerment for local people.
6. Respects local culture.
7. Supports human rights and democratic movements. (29–31)

While both definitions construct a view of ecotourism that is nature-based and sustainable while also helping to create income and empowerment for people who live in places with ecotourism sites, these definitions (as well as ecotourism generally) should also be seen as the antithesis to the large resort tourism that has proliferated, especially in Latin America and the Caribbean. For several decades, international aid agencies have pushed the idea of resort tourism as an economic development plan because of its ability to generate new income and employment. In many ways, ecotourism is a reaction to the large all-inclusive resort and seeks to be a more locally-integrated experience that engages with the environment and culture of the destination country.

While there is a lot of disagreement in the literature regarding precisely how ecotourism should be defined, the most important debate centers on whether or not ecotourism has lived up to its promise as a sustainable source of income for people in poor countries and the effect that ecotourism has on the destination country. The essence of the debate is not really over exactly what constitutes ecotourism, but instead the ability of nature-based tourism to create positive outcomes for those involved. The debate over ecotourism's effectiveness at achieving its goals revolves around its ramifications on the destination country's social fabric, politics and political institutions, economy, and natural environment. As such, it is important to assess the impact of ecotourism on more than just the economic lives of people, but how ecotourism affects their lives in a number of ways.

One of the most important critiques of ecotourism is its effects on the communities in which it takes place. These include the unequal economic relationship between ecotourists and the local population, the destruction of local cultures and customs brought on by an influx of foreigners and community changes due to the pursuit of tourist income. Due to these concerns, a lot of research has been devoted to the study of ecotourists and their attitudes, preferences, and interactions with people and the environment. One of the main promises of ecotourism is that it would create tourists who see the world differently and thus engage with local people in ways different from mass tourists. While mass tourists are happy to eat familiar food, socialize with familiar people while spending all their time at the resort, ecotourists are supposed to have a more adventurous streak and a stronger desire to engage with the local community. In addition, it is expected that ecotourists will be "greener" and thus more aware of and concerned with their own impact on the natural environment.

There is evidence that ecotourists are increasingly aware of their own impact and expect that ecotourism businesses engage in as many sustainable practices as possible and Andereck (2009) found that "nature tourists feel environmentally responsible business practices are more important and valuable than do other tourists." (493) As the idea of ecotourism has grown and matured, ecotourists have increasingly insisted on higher levels of environmental sustainability from tourism providers. In fact, rather than running roughshod over the people and natural environment of the destination country while on vacation, some studies have shown that ecotourists desire ever more sophisticated sustainability programs and are often displeased when the destination is not, in fact, green enough. In a study about ecotourism in Malaysia, Yusof, Said, and Rahman (2011) found that an ecotourist's expectations were not met with regard to the quality of the natural attractions, the integration with the natural environment, the resort's minimization of visitor's environmental impact and the utilization of recycling and reuse programs. (60) What is interesting about this study is that the ecotourists studied actually had higher expectations of their own ecotourism experience than the service providers were able (or willing) to give. These expectations are not surprising given that ecotourists tend to be middle-aged, willing to spend more money and time on their trip, and want to experience nature and see new things. They are also more likely to be members of environmental organizations. (Zografos and Allcroft 2007)

As such, ecotourism appears to have matured since the early days of the industry as it is tourists themselves that push ecotourism providers to offer services that are environmentally friendly and in line with what has been promised. The desire of ecotourists for sustainable ecotourism has led to the idea of demand-side approaches to reducing the ecological footprint of tourism. For the most part governments have tended to create supply-side approaches to sustainable ecotourism such as regulations on industry and the environment as well as ecotourism certification programs. Demand-side approaches on the other hand, "are based on the assumption that tourists have different ecological footprints and that the size of this footprint is a personal characteristic of each tourist and a function of how tourists behave environmentally during their visit." (Dolnicar, Crouch, and Long 2008, 199) As such, demand-side approaches attempt to guide tourists that are the most likely to have smaller ecological footprints to areas that are more environmentally fragile. While this approach is fraught with difficulties, the Costa Rican government has long used differential pricing to guide more or less tourists to different sites based on each site's ability to handle a set number of visitors. This is usually achieved through the use of differential pricing in which the more fragile parks charge a higher admission in hopes of driving tourists to other, less ecologically fragile areas. In a study of the use of this technique in Costa Rican national park system, Chase et al. (1998) found that:

> The estimated cross-price elasticities show that substitutability in visitation demand can exist between parks with similar attractions (e.g., the volcano parks). In cases such as this, charging differential fees (or increasing a preexisting fee differential) can effectively "push" tourists from one park to another, which may be desirable as part of a park management strategy to solve overcrowding at one park or to encourage local economic development at another. Other parks with unique characteristics, however, may not have readily available substitutes. Thus, changing entrance fees at the volcano parks will evidently have little impact on visitation at the beach park, and vice versa. (480)

Due to the need for substitute parks for this system to work, it works best in countries that have either a large national park system, a highly differentiated park system with several different types of parks available to tourists, or both. In addition, it is necessary that a differential pricing system be properly managed so that it achieves its goal of steering more tourists to less ecologically sensitive parks and away from those that cannot handle as many visitors. If not managed properly, any differential pricing system could easily make matters much worse. In addition, as tourist arrivals increase to a destination even a doubling of the price from \$10 to \$20 per person at a very famous park such as Manuel Antonio in Costa Rica might not easily dissuade ecotourists to go elsewhere to lesser known and less interesting parks.

Despite the desire on the part of ecotourists for their experience to adhere to certain levels of environmental sustainability, a further sign of maturity in the ecotourism market is demonstrated by an ecotourist's ability to contextualize their trip to the point of accepting some behaviors of the local population that are at odds with the tenets of ecotourism, particularly as it relates to subsistence and food security issues. For instance, Jones and Lalley (2013) found that "the main theme behind [ecotourists'] willingness to visit a reserve with subsistence hunting was the support of rural livelihoods with the stipulation that it be only for food security." (271) Obviously, hunting is a hot-button issue on ecotourism sites, particularly in preserves and national parks. Costa Rica, for instance, outlawed all hunting anywhere in the country in 2013. This was a logical step for Costa Rica since the number of subsistence hunters there was almost nil and the ban was seen as a boon to the ecotourism industry since hunting not only disturbs the ability to view wildlife, it will ultimately lead to its removal from the ecosystem. The willingness of ecotourists to tolerate hunting while on an ecotourism trip says a lot about their ability to understand the needs of the local population even as it is in conflict with the flora and fauna they traveled to see. This also shows a level of sophistication among ecotourists who are able to discern between their own needs as an ecotourist and needs of the local population for subsistence.

On the other hand, Rosaleen Duffy, who takes a very dim view of tourism in any form, in a study of ecotourists in Belize, found that ecotourists are almost indistinguishable from mass tourists and are motivated by self-indulgence and hedonism. She is also critical of ecotourists who view their holiday as "a chance to relax, let off steam and have a break from the constraints of their everyday existences in the industrialized states." (2002, 46) For scholars like Duffy, it is impossible to construct an equitable and effective ecotourism development plan because according to her "ecotourists and the ecotourism industry are causing environmental change, and a transformation in behavior is ultimately beyond the control of individual ecotourists." (45) It is interesting that Duffy would have such a negative view of ecotourists and their interaction with local people given that international travel is usually associated with opening one's mind and viewpoint to the perspectives of others and many universities include a study abroad component in their curriculum due to the relationship between international travel and education. In fact, best-selling travel writer Rick Steves observes that "the very people who would benefit most from international travel—those who needlessly fear people and places they don't understand—decide to stay home." (2015, 14) In this way tourism tends to be self-selecting, those who are less fearful and more open to new experiences are the most likely to travel abroad. Ecotourism shrinks this group even further as ecotourists tend to be the least fearful and the most open to new experiences given that the majority of ecotourism travel occurs within poor countries.

That is not to say of course that ecotourists are perfect, however they tend to have a much more well-defined sense of why they have traveled to a given location and have done so to experience, as much as possible, the full measure of a location. This is juxtaposed to a mass tourist who desires limited interactions and authenticity and in many respects wants a little bit of home to be recreated in a tropical location. Ecotourists by definition want to travel to experience something different and there is no reason to think that people from one country cannot travel to another country and treat the people there with respect or that if local people are treated with disrespect that they will be powerless against it. Horton (2009) in a study about Costa Rica found that the people there were perfectly capable of interacting with ecotourists on an equal basis and "in some instances, [ecotourism] has facilitated more sustained and more egalitarian interactions between local residents and ecotourists." (101) In many ways the idea that local populations in poor countries are helpless in the face of people from rich countries, is very unhelpful to the ability of poor countries to develop economically, since closing themselves off from the outside world is disastrous. When we travel, a big part of what we learn is that people are just people—be they Costa Rican, South African, Vietnamese, or whatever and not much different from ourselves.

Despite the positive effects of the inherent person-to-person interaction engendered by travel and tourism, there is a real danger that populations and locales can be overexposed to the practices of tourists and thus lose a part of their cultural identity. One of the chief paradoxes of tourism generally and ecotourism specifically is that visitors are drawn to "off-the-beaten-path" locales which then become mainstream, thus destroying the very thing that brought tourists in the first place. In addition, there is the risk that not only will more adventurous ecotourists move on to increasingly exotic places, but that the local community will begin to adopt the culture and practices of tourists, thus destroying the unique characteristics of the local population. This damages the community in two ways—via the destruction of local cultural traditions and the loss of tourist income garnered through those traditions. The danger, as stated by UNESCO is that "cultural industries can sometimes be harmful, exploiting local populations for global consumption, turning local values into tourist spectacles, commodifying cultural products without regard for the dignity of their producers." (2001, 11)

To combat these possibilities, it is important for states to utilize tourism policies that give local populations a stake in decision-making processes, because "if we nurture those cultural industries which deepen the ties between cultural values and cultural valuables, we can help local communities enter the global market without the sacrifice of either their dignity or their creativity." (UNESCO, 11) The nurturing and empowerment of these cultural industries will help to sustain them in the long term and will facilitate a more complete participation by various stakeholders. One of the best ways to cultivate local culture is to encourage local creativity rather than attempt to homogenize that culture into something that is perceived to be more palatable to tourists. According to Destination British Columbia, collaboration between cultural and tourism stakeholders works best under the following parameters.

1. Diverse parties who share a resource base work together.
2. The common effort results in a product that generates revenue for the local economy.
3. The product provides a quality tourism experience.
4. Increased use of the cultural heritage asset fosters appreciation by the local community and tourists alike. (2014, 16)

With these parameters in place, ecotourism can contribute to sociocultural conservation by accentuating the positive aspects of human interaction. The United Nations Environmental Programme found that tourism can contribute to human development by serving as a force for peace due to the importance of cultural exchange leading to better understanding. In addition, tourism can strengthen communities through the vitality inherent in cultural events and festivals developed to showcase local culture. This in turn can lead to the revaluation of cultural heritage and in some cases a renaissance of local heritage, cultural arts, and crafts. Finally, this continuation (or in some cases revival) of local cultural practice can encourage civic involvement and pride, which can motivate further conservation. (UNEP)

There has also been a lot of debate over ecotourism's ability to provide sustainable economic development, particularly for the poor, and the extent to which economic gains are spread across society. Given the myriad effects ecotourism can have across a number of hospitality service areas, its multiplier effect can be very large.

> Tourism is touted for having a three-pronged imprint on host economies, corresponding to its primary (direct) and secondary (indirect and induced) channels. Direct impacts accrue from initial tourist spending in the tourism industry—for instance, on hotel accommodations, transportation and entertainment. Indirect impacts are generated when tourist expenditures mainstream from the tourism economy to the general economy through purchases of goods and services from nontourist sectors of the local economy—for example, on food and beverages, equipment and furniture and merchandise. Finally, induced effects are attributable to the increased income of wage-earners related to the tourism economy, such as waiters, tour operators and construction workers, who in turn buy goods and services in the general economy. (Lejárraga and Walkenhorst 2010, 417)

Not only can ecotourism have an important multiplier effect on an economy, it also helps to increase a population's access to a variety of social services that help to aid in human development. In a study of Nicaragua, Croes (2012) found that "tourism growth expands capabilities directly, suggesting that as average tourism receipts increase, the population seems to have greater command over relevant resources (education, health, etc.) which leads to better human development performance. This connectivity is also mutually reinforcing: as human development performance improves, tourism services improve thereby yielding higher tourism revenues." (551) This is due in large part to the important link between the development of human capital and the success of ecotourism, which requires a populace capable of providing an educational element to arriving ecotourists and provides a health system and infrastructure that assists the population as well as ecotourists. It also shows that human capital development and expanded ecotourism activities are self-reinforcing.

While few would dispute that ecotourism, and tourism, generally, leads to higher incomes for the destination country, the real debate is over the extent to which these multiplier effects and human capital development have a direct positive impact on local people. For instance Coria and Calfucura (2012) find that "the distribution of the benefits of ecotourism reflects significant inequality between indigenous communities and external stakeholders." (54) Since much of what is considered ecotourism occurs in poor countries, it is very important to implement strategies that assist local people in being a part of the ecotourism industry to make certain that the very poorest people in the destination country are able to benefit from development. One of the major challenges of ecotourism development is to minimize the extent of economic leakage, which is the amount of money that does not remain "in-country" as a result of a tourism-based economic activity. Economic leakage can be particularly acute in the tourism industry since a large amount of the money paid for a trip often goes to companies outside the destination country. For instance, the economic impact of someone booking a trip in which they stay in a locally owned hotel and eat in local restaurants differs from a trip in which people stay at the Hilton and eat at American chain restaurants. The extent to which there is economic leakage in the tourism industry is another of the major differences between ecotourism which exists as a community-based activity and mass tourism which interacts very little with anybody or anything "off-resort." At the extreme end of the spectrum, there are even examples of destinations that have banned tourists from buying anything outside the confines of the resort. (Freitag 1994)

The primary cause of economic leakage is the lack of investment capital in the destination country, which leads to the development of only a small number of locally owned businesses providing tourism services. The lack of locally owned businesses also leads to lack of employment for local people across multiple skill levels. In addition, economic leakage occurs when there are few linkages between the local tourism industry and the broader economy as food and other supplies are imported from the outside. These problems are more acute in poor countries as a much higher percentage of income is lost to economic leakage than it is the developed world. For example, Diaz (2001) found that "the average leakage for most developing countries today is between 40 and 50 percent of gross tourism earnings for small economies and between 10 and 20 percent for most advanced and diversified developing countries." (8) This is not surprising, since the money lost to developed countries through economic leakage is buying products in the developed world, while tourism companies in the developed buy those same products from the same suppliers which are in their own country.

Unemployment as well as underemployment also contributes to economic leakage at ecotourism destinations because oftentimes tourism-related jobs, particularly higher-skilled jobs, are not performed by people from the local population. Choudhury and Goswami (2013) in a study of Manas National Park in India found that a significant percentage of skilled tourism jobs were held by nonlocal staff, reflecting either a lack of local individuals with the appropriate skills or a reluctance to hire them. (75) In many ways, problems of economic leakage are self-reinforcing as lack of capital leads to low levels of employment for local people in the tourism industry who then do not gain the requisite experience to open their own tourism-related business, which in turn would be able to provide capital for the local community.

In order to break the cycle that leads to a high percentage of economic leakage in a destination country, policy makers must concentrate on options that encourage an expansion of ecotourism because "tourism expansion invariably creates demand in a broad array of economic sectors in the host economy, generating new supply opportunities for existing and emerging products. These opportunities may be captured locally or internationally, depending on the extent of linkages and leakages that characterize the relationship between the tourism economy and the general economy." (Lejárraga and Walkenhorst 2010, 417) One of the best ways to spread the multiplier effect throughout the economy is by policy makers also concentrating on policies that will boost local ownership and employment in the ecotourism sector.

One of the reasons that Costa Rica has been able to benefit from ecotourism is that they were able to develop a lot of locally owned ecotourism-related businesses just as the industry was starting to take off in the 1970s and 1980s, particularly at ecotourism sites that are away from the coastline. Due to the focus on local ownership early in the development of Costa Rican ecotourism, many of the businesses that are considered ecotourism in Costa Rica are Costa Rican–owned. Conversely, due to patterns of development on the coast, the large resorts there tend to be foreign-owned, many by

Americans and are often guilty of a high rate of economic leakage. Due to the sort of visitors that are attracted to resorts, "foreign ownership and management of tourist facilities generally rely heavily on imported goods and services, higher proportions of foreign employees, and minimal linkages to other local economic sectors like agriculture and light industry." (Moreno 2005, 238)

One of the most interesting aspects of ecotourism is that since ecotourists tend to favor a more local experience, the higher the level of participation by local people (and thus the lower the level of economic leakage) the higher the level of satisfaction reported by many ecotourists. Galdon, Garrigos, and Gil-Pechuan (2013) found that "an entrepreneurial environment, measured as a low level of leakage directly and positively affects improvements in employee and customer satisfaction, thereby enhancing company competitiveness." (768) This is not surprising given what we know about the preferences of ecotourists, since many report preferences for a local experience.

Some scholars also argue that ecotourism has negative effects on poor countries due to its association with globalization and neoliberalism. For instance, Duffy (2008) argues that "the focus on ecotourism results in the further extension of neoliberalism into new areas, which may in turn have negative impacts on the very groups they were intended to benefit." (341) Despite some rhetorical misgivings regarding globalization, neoliberalism and direct foreign investment, states across Latin America pursue outside investment in order to build their economies and most actively pursue opportunities that emerge from openness to the global economy. Even states that appear to oppose open markets, often still pursue foreign investment. For instance, Montero (2008) writes, "there is not a single Latin American country, including Cuba, that is not actively wooing foreign firms to open new subsidiaries or to expand existing operations in their economies." (55) While ecotourism development is not a panacea that will solve all of the economic problems present in poor countries, it provides an outstanding strategy for development. Not only is tourism listed as an important lever for poverty reduction in the United Nations Millennium Declaration, but according to the World Tourism Organization it is a major job generator for the world's most vulnerable people. (UNWTO 2013, 3–4) Ecotourism is uniquely positioned to assist in economic development because tourism activities by their nature are only able to occur "in-country." This fact alone holds great promise for local entrepreneurship, employment, and linkages to the broader economy. In addition, many states across Latin America and the Caribbean that need economic development the most are the same ones that have many of the ecological characteristics necessary for a successful ecotourism industry.

Politically, the debate over the effect of ecotourism on a destination country is often the extent to which poor countries lose a portion of their sovereignty as they attempt to attract ecotourism investment, particularly from large multinational corporations. This is especially problematic in countries that rely heavily on direct foreign investment for large portions of its capital. The development of ecotourism in Costa Rica starting in the 1970s provides an excellent example of the positive effects of combining ecotourism development with direct foreign investment. Early ecotourism development in Costa Rica was encouraged by government policies in two areas: the preservation of protected areas, which gave ecotourism a place to exist, and tax policies that encouraged ecotourism entrepreneurship. The combination of these two areas, helped Costa Rica to develop a viable ecotourism industry in the 1970s and 1980s and by the 1990s was a major source of foreign exchange. Costa Rica was able to take areas that are often divergent e.g. development and environmentalism and combine them into ecotourism. They were able to do this because "in Costa Rica, sovereignty, democracy and the environment are intertwined." (Graef 2013, 285)

Furthermore, Costa Rica was able to develop its ecotourism industry by opening itself to the outside world and encouraging local operators to service the incoming ecotourists. One of the most important lessons that can be learned from the Costa Rican experience is that ecotourism development must work alongside other more traditional forms of development, for instance agriculture, in order to create a more diversified set of economic activities. In addition, Costa Rica illustrates the importance of developing a society-wide environmental ethic that can guide the relationship between ecotourism and other industries. Long before Costa Rica developed its ecotourism industry, the Costa Rican environmental movement had won concessions from the government that helped to create a situation in which the "legal, institutional, and administrative mechanisms and capacities, which were already in place and subsequently refashioned further under a string of governments supporting neoliberal-style economic and political policies, are recognized as having fueled the national conservation boom of Costa Rica." (Zimmerer 2011, 92)

Another important aspect of ecotourism development is its interaction with the natural environment and the ways in which ecotourism may or may not support sustainability. In many ways the most controversial critique of ecotourism is that it subordinates the environment to the generation of income and therefore is not fulfilling its promise of sustainability. For instance, West and Carrier (2004) argue that ecotourism creates pressure for states to "[subordinate] concern for environmental conservation and respect for local communities, which ecotourism is said to encourage, to concern for attracting ecotourists and their money." (491) The idea that the environment "loses out" to profit because of ecotourism is common in the scholarly literature. This idea is often connected to the idea that ecotourism development in partner with neoliberal capitalism pollutes an environment and people that would otherwise be faithful stewards of the land. In fact, for many scholars sustainability and capitalism are simply irreconcilable. For instance, Hames (1991) argues that the most "devastating change in aboriginal environmental relations is when people move away from subsistence agriculture and into a market-based economy in order to make a living." (192)

Another potential environmental problem in ecotourism is that it can adversely affect an area by being too successful. This can mean both that too many tourists overrun the area causing stress to the environment or that economic success can lead to the area being overpopulated as people who live in the country descend on the successful ecotourism site as they are acutely aware of the economic benefits of living in and around an area with a vibrant ecotourism industry. In a study of the Galapagos Islands, Taylor et al. (2003) found that increased tourism revenue led to increased migration to the ecotourism area equal to 5 percent of the island workforce for every 10 percent increase in tourism revenue, potentially leading to environmental strain based not on the ecotourists, but on those that seek employment in ecotourism areas that are experiencing economic growth. In addition, they found that there is a strong complementarity between tourism, and environmentally sensitive island production activities, including agriculture and livestock, fishing and other types of natural resource extraction. (993)

Ecotourists also have a preference for an educational component to their trip and studies have shown that providing even a minimal level of education on minimizing the impact on the environment has a positive effect. For instance, Marion and Reid (2007) found that there is adequate evidence that most of the visitor education methods evaluated did affect visitor knowledge, attitudes, behavior, and/or resource conditions in the intended direction. Some efforts did not achieve their stated goals for various reasons, but the majority of educational efforts succeeded in altering visitor behavior (18) On this note, one of the best positive effects of ecotourism is its ability to engage visitors in a deeper understanding of ecology and sustainability. Powell and Ham (2008) found that "[ecotourism] is capable of increasing tourists' philanthropic support of conservation as well as positively influencing their knowledge and attitudes towards protected areas and general environmental behavioural [*sic*] intentions." (484)

Not surprisingly, the relationship between sustainable ecotourism development and the environment is largely an issue of how it is implemented in a society and economy, especially the extent to which policies are in place that will help to minimize negative impacts. Due to this, "tourism remains arguably the commercial enterprise most likely to work in harmony with conservation objectives, as long as the impacts can be minimized." (Vaughan 2000, 196) On balance, ecotourism has been a success for states and communities that have utilized it as a source of foreign exchange. Many of the ecotourism detractors base their critiques on the imperfectability of ecotourism while many ecotourism celebrants fail to adequately deal with the parts of it that need to be fixed. In addition, ecotourism detractors tend to focus on ecotourism's relationship to global capitalism and globalization, which they see at face value as a negative. One of the most interesting parts of ecotourism is that so much of the argument regarding its efficacy is either all or nothing.

> While proponents see in ecotourism the potential to advance income-generating opportunities, environmental conservation, and local empowerment, critics suggest that as (Latin America's) latest transnational, market-driven process ecotourism perpetuates historical economic inequalities and further disempowers local peoples. On the Osa Peninsula, ecotourism has fulfilled neither these worst fears nor the most optimistic of hopes. (Horton 2009, 103–4)

SUSTAINABLE ECOTOURISM

Despite the disputed nature of ecotourism and its many variants, some consensus has begun to emerge around the idea of "sustainable tourism" as the appropriate paradigm from which to understand the relationship between sustainability and tourism activities. The World Tourism Organization defines sustainable tourism as "tourism that takes full account of its current and future economic, social and environmental impacts, addressing the needs of visitors, the industry, the environment and host communities" (UNWTO) The transition from "ecotourism" to "sustainable tourism" can be traced to an increased focus on the concept of sustainable development as laid out by the World Commission on Environment and Development (WCED) in *Our Common Future* which conceptualizes sustainable development as development that meets the needs of the present without compromising the ability of future generations to meet their own needs. (1987, 43)

The merger of ecotourism and sustainability is of the utmost importance because both are vitally important to developing states. Ecotourism can attract tourists to a destination, while concepts of sustainability can ensure that the destinations remain viable sources of income for generations. LePree (2008–2009) argues that:

> The most widely held assumptions concerning the difference between sustainable tourism and ecotourism are that sustainable tourism as a minimum must meet the definition of sustainable development that was posited in *Our Common Future*, namely to be an activity that will be able to be practiced by future generations without handicaps or limitations due to the actions of the current generation, whereas ecotourism should meet the above definition and in addition include some type of interpretive experience of the local ecology. (54)

For their part, many states, including Costa Rica, no longer use the term *ecotourism* and have begun to call these activities *sustainable tourism*. In

Costa Rica, the term is meant to signify the coalescence of the nature-based aspects of ecotourism with policies and standards to increase sustainability. Costa Rica, one of the pioneers of the idea of ecotourism, has also expanded its use of mass tourism, thus necessitating dropping the "eco" from tourism. Hopefully, neglecting the "eco" part of ecotourism will mean that traditional tourism will become more eco-friendly rather than ecotourism becoming less. The change in Costa Rica from promoting ecotourism activities to the promotion of more traditional forms of tourism is discussed in chapter 1.

Due to the centrality of tourism to the economies of many poor countries and the need to perpetuate the tourism industry via sustainability, merging the ideas inherent in ecotourism and sustainability into a single policy concept is vital to long-term economic development and environmental sustainability in many poor countries. As such, states would be well advised to concentrate their tourism development efforts around the ideas of sustainable ecotourism. Sustainable ecotourism should be nature-based, sustainable, educational, and profitable while ensuring that it will continue to be for future generations. While it seems simple that anything that contains the prefix "eco" would be nature-based, the characterization of activities which take place in nature but are not really nature-based, such as going to the beach should not be included in a definition of sustainable ecotourism. One of the best ways to make sure that activities deemed "sustainable ecotourism" have an actual nature-based component is for them to also have an educational component. An educational component to ecotourism also helps people to build an environmental awareness that can then perpetuate sustainable ecotourism. Successful sustainable ecotourism that is nature-based and educational will also have a much better chance of being sustainable as it will tend to attract ecotourists that leave a smaller environmental footprint and who will be more interested in conservation. The bulk of what needs to be done regarding sustainability does not emanate from the ecotourist, but instead from those that are providing hotels, rental cars, excursions and food at a destination. It is also important for sustainable ecotourism to have an educational element so that ecotourists can learn about and interact with the natural world. While very common among many different types of ecotourism ventures, the educational element is often the key to attracting ecotourists to a destination and often leads to a much higher level of satisfaction with the trip. For instance, in a study of Belize, Kwan, Eagles, and Gebhardt (2008) found that ecotourism attracts a highly educated clientele whose highest motivation for the trip was the desire to see the wilderness and undisturbed nature.

One aspect that many scholars have often neglected to include in any definition of ecotourism is the necessity for it to be profitable. It is important for ecotourism to be profitable because economic gains from ecotourism will help to perpetuate it and will make entrepreneurs more interested in nature-based and educational sustainable ecotourism. In addition, profitability helps to give the environment a political voice because of its contributions to national incomes. A big part of what has made ecotourism a major source of income in Costa Rica is the early development of an ecotourism industry that was able to push for laws that helped to preserve the environment. The relationship between the money-making aspects and preservation of the environment is the key to understanding the need for profitability in ecotourism. Unlike industrial development, the logic of ecotourism is that it needs to preserve the environment because it is the very place in which business is conducted. If ecotourism does not preserve the natural environment, ecotourism itself will cease to exist.

ECOTOURISM CERTIFICATION PROGRAMS

Due to many of the issues discussed above and the difficulty in defining ecotourism and the myriad number of activities that can be construed as such, it is important for states, and increasingly international organizations, to utilize ecotourism certification to assure consumers that operations are actually engaged in the sustainable practices that they claim. Yusof, Said, and Rahman (2011) argue that problems inherent in defining ecotourism have led "to difficulties in establishing quality standards for the industry." (52) One of the ways to better define sustainable ecotourism and the activities it encompasses is to arrive at a standard definition that is verifiable via a rigorous certification process by an outside organization. Ecotourism certification programs are "voluntary instruments to improve the environmental, social and economic performance of tourism companies; they offer trade and marketing advantages to certified firms, provide credible information to suppliers and consumers, and encourage more sustainable consumption." (Font 2007, 401) Due to the desire of many ecotourists to utilize environmentally sustainable facilities "the vast majority of certification programmes [*sic*] in tourism focus on the concept of sustainable tourism." (Kroshus Medina 2005, 282) While the awareness of sustainability issues is increasing generally, it is even more prominent among those who travel to view and experience unique ecological features. The sensitivity of ecotourists to sustainability issues is logical since they are traveling out of their comfort zone, and sometimes off the beaten path, in order to view a natural feature they cannot see at home. Ecotourism and/or sustainability certification programs give tourists the ability to patronize businesses that have been certified by a third party as being sensitive to sustainability issues.

The growth in popularity of ecotourism certification programs is due not only to increasing demand from ecotourists, most of whom tend to be older, more educated, and able to spend more money on their trip, but also because of the pressure put on ecotourism firms by the government to participate in certification schemes. For instance, Rivera (2004) found that "[ecotourism certification] appears to require the complement of coercive institutional pressures in the form of government environmental monitoring and normative pressures arising from industry association membership." (792) Many ecotourism providers desire certification to differentiate themselves from other providers who merely pay lip service to sustainability. For instance, "the demand for some well-established sustainable tourism programs [Australia, Costa Rica, Quebec] came from hoteliers and tour operators who were sincerely committed to sound sustainability, environmental, ecological, and socioeconomic practices (but) faced what they perceived as unfair competition from 'cowboys' or 'greenwashers,' who claimed similar practices but had taken no concrete action." (Toth 2002, 97)

Despite the idea that globalization and neoliberalism has pushed the state out of the picture, ecotourism certification programs hold a lot of promise because of their ability to include a large number of stakeholders. For instance, Honey and Stewart (2002) argue that "certification programs provide an effective tool because, unlike many of the other initiatives [used to regulate ecotourism] they can meet and balance the needs and interests of a variety of stakeholders." (51) As such, this is a policy area in which the state can play an important role. One of the most important ecotourism certification programs in the world the Costa Rican government's Certificate for Sustainable Tourism (CST) given by the *Instituto Costarricense de Turismo* (ICT). Despite its status as a developing country, Costa Rica's management of ecotourism and the ICT is widely seen as a leader in the field. For instance, Silva (2003) argues that "opinion leaders around the world see [Costa Rica] as a leader and pioneer in community forestry, bioprospecting, 'green' taxes, carbon emissions trading, and administrative decentralization in managing protected areas." (93) The Costa Rican ecotourism industry takes certification by the ICT very seriously and a high rating is greatly prized. Once an ecotourism business is rated, the CST logo is usually displayed on its front door and mentioned on its website. While the natural environment would benefit from ecotourism businesses adhering to models of sustainability, the effectiveness of the CST is enhanced if it helps to direct tourists to CST certified operations.

The CST certifies the degree to which ecotourism companies comply with a sustainable model of natural, cultural and social resource management. It accomplishes this through a comprehensive checklist of items for both ecotourism agencies and hotels, including the assessment of things such as emissions and the protection of flora and fauna. (*Certificación para la Sostenibilidad Turística*) As a world leader in sustainability policy, Costa Rican leadership on ecotourism certification programs is important to the global development of the ability to measure the standards of ecotourism against a defined set of principles. For instance, the CST was adopted by the International Organization for Standardization which established a committee on tourism standardization in concert with the Costa Rican government. (Mowforth and Munt 2009, 205)

In order for an operation to receive CST certification they are evaluated within four parameters. Within each of these parameters, businesses are given a ranking of one to five green leaves.

1. *Physical-biological interactions*
   Evaluates the interaction between the company and its surrounding natural habitat.
2. *Infrastructure and services*
   Evaluates the management policies and operational systems within the company and its infrastructure.
3. *External clients*
   Evaluates management actions taken in its invitation to clients to participate in the company's sustainability policy implementation.
4. *Socioeconomic environment*
   Evaluates the company's interaction with local communities and population in general. (CST)

Part of what makes the CST a more successful certification structure is that it concentrates its certification efforts on performance rather than on process. While process-based certification focuses on the use of environmental management systems, performance based systems focus on sociocultural and economic criteria or benchmarks. (Honey and Stewart 2002, 53) Performance based systems are more successful because they measure the actual outcomes of environmental management rather than simply making certain environmental management techniques are in place. Due to this, process-based systems provide perfect cover for large chains who want to have the benefit of having environmentally sensitive measures in place while not actually having anyone measure whether or not what they are doing is successful.

While the number of Costa Rican hotels that apply for and receive certification is on the rise, in the last decade Costa Rica's increasing reliance on large foreign-owned resorts for development has somewhat mitigated the use of the CST. In many ways the presence of these large-scale foreign owned resorts is the antithesis to ecotourism's focus on small-scale community-oriented tourism activities. Despite these large international hotel chains having far more resources at their disposal and also often pay a great deal of lip service to sustainability, research indicates that large multinational hotel chains "do not exhibit significantly higher participation and superior environmental performance in the CST program than locally owned firms." (Rivera 2004, 793)

GLOBALIZATION, NEOLIBERALISM, AND SUSTAINABLE ECOTOURISM

In a well-known article from *Harvard Business Review*, Theodore Levitt declares that "a powerful force drives the world toward a converging commonality, and that force is technology. It has proletarianized communication, transport, and travel." (1983, 92) This globalized "proletarianization" of communication, transport, and travel has been a boon for the tourism industry and has made it one of the world's most important economic activities. It is estimated that there were 1.1 billion international tourists in 2014 with the largest amount of growth (8 percent over the previous year) in the Americas. (UNWTO 2015) What is interesting about the effectiveness of sustainable ecotourism (or tourism generally) in generating income for poor countries is that the large number of international travelers was achieved despite the fact that, according to UNWTO Secretary-General Taleb Rifai "different parts of the world continue to face significant geopolitical and health challenges [and] while the global economic recovery remains rather fragile and uneven." (UNWTO 2015) As such, sustainable ecotourism can provide a form of development that is somewhat immune to global downturns and is often one of the first sectors to bounce back in the aftermath of a recession. This is due in large part to the many ways in which globalization has integrated and shrunk the world and the ease of both finding information regarding vacation destinations and booking trips to those locations. In addition, globalization has made travel easier for tourists once they have arrived at a destination due to myriad technologies such as bank networks, global positioning systems (GPS) for navigation in a rental car and communications technology to name a few.

The International Monetary Fund (IMF) (2000) defines globalization as "a historical process, the result of human innovation and technological progress. It refers to the increasing integration of economies around the world, particularly through trade and financial flows. The term sometimes also refers to the movement of people (labor) and knowledge (technology) across international borders. At the center of the relationship between globalization and ecotourism is the extent to which globalization helps to create economic, social, and political convergence and the ways in which this convergence makes the development of an ecotourism industry viable. Particularly important is the integration and convergence created by what the IMF (2000) refers to as the four aspects of globalization: trade, capital movements, movement of people, and the spread of knowledge and technology.

These four aspects of globalization facilitate sustainable ecotourism because utilizing any type of tourism as a development strategy works best in a modern, globalized and integrated economy. In addition, sustainable ecotourism can help generate income from outside the country in ways that are similar to income derived from international trade. While sustainable ecotourism is not "trade" in the literal sense, it mimics the effects of trade because it seeks to generate income from outside the host country for goods and services created therein. Croes and Vanegas (2008) write "considering that all international tourism demand generates foreign exchange earnings in contrast to other sectors, [a domestic ecotourism market] is the equivalent of Nicaragua exporting tourism goods and services to be consumed by foreigners in their countries." (101) In this way sustainable ecotourism can help to alleviate one of the most common critiques of globalization—that it increases the need for states to compete in the international market via agricultural exports to the developed world. In fact, given that there are many comparative advantages for the development of sustainable ecotourism across Latin America and the Caribbean these strategies allow poor states to better compete with their wealthier counterparts. They are also able to compete in a world in which potential ecotourists can plan an entire trip from their living room sofa due to our globalized world and those trips then have a similar economic effect to export industries. This has meant that poor states can "export" services to the outside world that require no industrial development.

The movement of capital is also important to the development of sustainable ecotourism because of the necessity in many poor countries for outside investment in order to establish a viable ecotourism industry. In addition, capital mobility helps states to create a development plan that encourages foreign direct investment across a number of areas of the economy. Not only does this increase the chances of economic development, but also helps to move poor states away from the reliance on a small number of economic activities—many of which subject poor states to a great deal of economic risk. In addition, one of the most important aspects of any form of tourism is for potential visitors to have the ability to easily move around the globe with very few restrictions. As such, one of the most important aspects of globalization's focus on the mobility of people is the ability to send people all over the globe in pursuit of tourism activities. The increased ability for people to travel in our globalized world is also aided by the manner in which knowledge and technology is also spread around the globe.

This spread of knowledge and technology is the key to understanding how sustainable ecotourism and globalization can fit together because of the need for information on the part of potential ecotourists and the potential for technology to make travel planning much simpler, particularly to far-flung parts of the world which are often the places that need economic development the most. At its minimum, modern communications technology opens up parts of the world to ecotourism that had previously been difficult for tourists to plan due a lack of information and helps to create ecotourism demand for places that until recently had been seen as off the beaten path. One of the most intriguing aspects of the manner in which globalization and ecotourism intersect is people can more easily learn about and plan travel to places in the world that only a couple decades would have been much more difficult.

While the globalization literature has been voluminous—with many scholars wary of the effects of globalization on both poor and wealthy states, in essence the era of discussing whether globalization could or should be embraced by policy makers and governments is over as globalization is inevitable and unstoppable. This does not mean that governments cannot manage globalization and its effects on their country, but instead that globalization should be embraced and used to enhance the economic, political, and social development of poor states. Since globalization is here to stay, policy makers need to consider sustainable ecotourism policies that engage with the globalized world in a way that also spreads the benefit to as many people as possible.

The interaction between globalization and sustainable ecotourism creates a number of positive conditions for the host country. The first is an increase in employment and income predicated on the expansion of sustainable ecotourism. In addition, sustainable ecotourism creates important linkages to other industries such as food production and creates an important multiplier effect that can help to spread income across an economy. The relationship between ecotourism and agriculture is especially important as oftentimes the two industries are at odds with one another since agriculture often expands into areas needed for ecotourism and vice versa. The linkage between the two also provides important links between a traditional economic enterprise (agriculture) and a new one (sustainable ecotourism). For instance, Costa Rica has been able to take its most well-known agricultural product, coffee, and use it in both ecotourism and agro-tourism and coffee farms and other coffee-related enterprises have become tourists attractions on their own. In addition, since sustainable ecotourism seeks to create a nature-based experience that is deeply embedded in its locale, the linkage between tourism activities and locally grown food is very strong. Finally, developing an ecotourism industry will help to improve local empowerment which will assist in the development of entrepreneurship.

Another important reason for community involvement and local empowerment is to minimize the extent to which globalized tourism alters the social fabric of the community. Part of the problem is how something is kept off the beaten path yet developed in such a way that it contributes to the economic development of the area. With the changes brought about by globalization and most importantly by globalized tourism it is essential that as many stakeholders as possible are brought into the process so that people feel as though are benefiting from the development of sustainable ecotourism and have a voice in its direction.

While globalization represents one important ingredient for the development of sustainable ecotourism, the other is the rise of neoliberalism in the time after World War II. The basis of neoliberalism is built on ideas of private property, markets, competition and limited state intervention in the economy and as Milton Friedman (1962) argues the "elementary proposition that both parties to an economic transaction benefit from it, provided the transaction is bilaterally voluntary and informed." (55) In many ways tourism and modern neoliberal capitalism are inextricable linked due to the need for economic integration, the spread of information and the freedom of movement among tourists traveling in a foreign country. Bianchi (2007) states that "the direct association between travel, freedom and consumption has arguably reached its zenith under the contemporary conditions of neoliberal capitalism." (65) Many of the factors that make sustainable ecotourism development attractive to states also helps states to attract foreign direct investment. These include an open economy, educated populace, and an infrastructure that makes travel in and around the country easy as well as a government that facilitates the rule of law.

The founding moment of neoliberalism came at the Walter Lippman *Colloque* held in Paris in 1938. The *colloque* was organized by French philosopher Louis Rougier to discuss Lippman's ideas regarding collectivist versus market economies from his new book *The Good Society* published the previous year. At the *colloque* "a number of leading market liberal intellectuals, including [Friedrich] Hayek and [Ludwig von] Mises, debated the agenda for a revived liberalism proposed by Lippman in *The Good Society*." (Jackson 2012, 58) The idea among the participants was to create a new form of economic liberalism to replace the old laissez-faire variety practiced for much of the previous century and had been perceived as a failure. After a lot of debate, "the [participants] were united in their call for a new liberal project—a project that still needed a name. 'Liberalism from the left' was one idea; others were 'positive liberalism' or 'social liberalism.' But the term on which the participants actually agreed upon was 'neoliberalism.'" (Hartwich 2009, 19)

Much of the discussion at the *colloque* centered on the role of the state in the economy as the arbiter of competition among private enterprise with a lot of debate among the participants. For some at the *colloque*, such as Hayek and (especially) Mises even a minimal amount of state intervention was too much. Not surprisingly, this hardline stance created a rift between Hayek, Mises and the rest of the group with Mises at one point storming out and accusing everyone at the meeting of being socialists. (21) What is particularly interesting about the form of neoliberalism that came out of the *colloque* is that it was not the "minimum state" written about by Hayek, but instead gave the state a role to play, particularly in ensuring that firms have an even competitive playing field. "The neoliberalism that came out of the Colloque

Walter Lippmann was much in line with Rüstow's political and economic theories. It was no longer a conception of unrestricted liberty, but a market economy under the guidance and the rules of the state. To quote Rüstow's seminal 1932 speech, it was the idea of both a free economy and a strong state." (19)

Picking up on this in 1951, economist Milton Friedman expounded on the primary rationale for neoliberalism (a term Friedman himself rarely used), by putting the focus on competition and the state's role in ensuring that markets remain in perpetual competition.

> Neo-liberalism would accept the nineteenth century liberal emphasis on the fundamental importance of the individual, but it would substitute for the nineteenth century goal of laissez-faire as a means to this end, the goal of the competitive order. It would seek to use competition among producers to protect consumers from exploitation, competition among employers to protect workers and owners of property, and competition among consumers to protect the enterprises themselves. The state would police the system, establish conditions favorable to competition and prevent monopoly, provide a stable monetary framework, and relieve acute misery and distress. The citizens would be protected against the state by the existence of a free private market; and against one another by the preservation of competition. (Friedman 1951, 91)

For Friedman, competition is the key factor in balancing markets and protecting citizens from harm. It is important to note that Friedman, like the majority at the *colloque*, saw the role of the state as the ultimate enforcer of competition among the various players, which is somewhat at odds with the modern conception of neoliberalism seemingly opposed to any type of state intervention. In many ways the modern incarnation of neoliberalism is a return to the more doctrinaire version advocated by Hayek and Mises at the *collogue* as channeled through US President Ronald Reagan and British Prime Minister Margaret Thatcher in the 1980s and came to be known as the "New Right."

While it would take thirty years for Hayek's ideas to influence politics and economics, both Reagan and Thatcher attached great importance to Hayek's ideas on the centrality of liberty in economics. In fact,

> the emergence of the New Right and the strength of doctrines of neoliberalism throughout the 1970s and 1980s and their espousal by influential political leaders and political movements in many countries signified the triumph of Hayek's lonely crusade. From a position of great isolation and apparent irrelevance in the 1940s, he found himself thirty years later the acknowledged leader of the new political orthodoxy, the intellectual guide of prime ministers and presidents, the icon of a rapidly growing world-wide movement, and the recipient of numerous honours, [*sic*] including the Nobel Prize for Economics. (Gamble 1996, 10)

Thatcher and Reagan found the ideas inherent in neoliberalism attractive as they each came to power during times of upheaval and uncertainty in much of the world. "The dramatic consolidation of neoliberalism as a new economic orthodoxy regulating public policy at the state level in the advanced industrial world occurred in the United States and Britain in 1979" (Harvey 2005, 22) As policy makers in the United States and Britain turned to neoliberal economic ideas at home, they each also started to exports those same ideas abroad via what has come to be known as the Washington Consensus.

Subject to much debate and no small amount of ridicule, the Washington Consensus has been controversial since John Williamson named it such in 1990. The Washington Consensus is a set of ten "lowest common denominator" economic policies based on the ides of neoliberalism for encouraging growth in the developing world. These ten policies are:

1. Fiscal discipline.
2. A redirection of public expenditure priorities toward fields offering both high economic returns and the potential to improve income distribution, such as primary health care, primary education, and infrastructure.
3. Tax reform (to lower marginal rates and broaden the tax base).
4. Interest rate liberalization.
5. A competitive exchange rate.
6. Trade liberalization.
7. Liberalization of FDI inflows.
8. Privatization.
9. Deregulation (in the sense of abolishing barriers to entry and exit).
10. Secure property rights. (Williamson 1990)

As Williamson (2002) points out "audiences the world over seem to believe that [the Washington Consensus] signifies a set of neoliberal policies that have been imposed on hapless countries by the Washington-based international financial institutions and have led them to crisis and misery. There are people who cannot utter the term without foaming at the mouth." Indeed the backlash against neoliberalism as expressed in the Washington Consensus has been fierce, with many of its harshest critics arguing that far from being the treatment for poverty in the developing world, it has instead been the cause of increased poverty. For instance, Joseph Stiglitz, one of the biggest critics of the Washington Consensus states that "the results of the policies enforced by the Washington Consensus have not been encouraging: for the most countries embracing its tenets development has been slow, and where growth has occurred, the benefits have not been shared equally." (2003, 86)

From a mistrust in markets and the desire to shape the world in the way they see fit with as much government planning as possible, many academics, policy makers (particularly in the developing world), and increasingly decision makers at international financial institutions have turned to a new set of ideas knows as the "post–Washington Consensus" which seeks to bring the state back to prominence. This includes managing trade and monetary systems, increasing the social safety net, and imposing regulations on the market. These measures are largely used to protect people from the international market and therefore from what some consider to be the undesirable effects of competition.

Given the globalized world, government and policy makers have a role to play in ensuring that their state is competitive in the world market by formulating policies that open their markets to the outside world while also encouraging local entrepreneurship. Another way that governments and policy makers can help to ensure their country is competitive in the world tourism market is through having a sufficient rule of law so that people feel comfortable visiting. While this will certainly be difficult, violence and instability will make it very hard for states to compete for tourists. Another way for states to boost their competitiveness for sustainable ecotourism in the world market is by having an infrastructure that is suitable for incoming visitors. In addition, the case studies in this book have the added advantage of being geographically close to the large number of potential visitors from the United States and Canada. For sustainable ecotourism to thrive, this must all be done within the context of environmental protection and sustainability. The crucial point is to utilize nature-based tourism in such a way that people can improve their lives in the present without compromising that same asset so that others may use it in the future.

COMPARATIVE ADVANTAGES OF SUSTAINABLE ECOTOURISM

Globalization and neoliberalism allow poor states to pursue the development of sustainable ecotourism based on a set of comparative advantages that set them apart from others. Unlike most other areas of the international economy, poor states can easily compete with richer states for tourism dollars. In particular, sustainable ecotourism presents a unique opportunity for poor states to compete for tourists as they contain many of the world's most unique ecotourism sites and destinations. The most important comparative advantage of the countries discussed in this book, as well as throughout Central America and the Caribbean is their ability to deliver value to visiting ecotourists. Each country also has a unique set of attributes that set them apart from other ecotourism destinations, when coupled with their ability to deliver value giving them many advantages over many other places around the world, particularly in the developed world. The unique attributes in each country includes things such as the Panama Canal, surfing and Ometepe Island in Nicaragua, and the Blue Hole of Belize. In addition, each country has a unique culture, people, and cuisine that all serve to attract visitors. Given the proximity of Panama, Nicaragua, and Belize to the major North American market, the ease of travel is also an important comparative advantage. Finally, the extent to which each state has an open economy that makes travel easy for visitors is also a significant comparative advantage as it is important for states to be open and integrated into the world market so visitors have access to their money via cash machines and/or have the ability to use a credit card as well as access to communications technology to keep in touch with their relatives at home.

Chapter One

Ecotourism in Costa Rica

Since the mid-1980s, Costa Rica has been considered among the most important ecotourism destinations in the world. Costa Rica was able to take its nature-based attractions, which are among some of the most interesting in the world and parlay them into a major part of their economy due to long-term political and social stability, a good tourist infrastructure, an open economy, and an educated populace. These attributes were further enriched by the cultivation of Costa Rica as a high-value destination, particularly for American tourists who might otherwise travel to Europe or Hawai'i. The World Bank Reports that in 2013 tourism represented 18.2 percent of Costa Rican exports for a total expenditure of US$2.82 billion. Costa Rica has also been very successful in attracting foreign direct investment, with investment inflows of US$3.28 billion in 2013 and US$2.345 billion in 2014. (World Bank)

As a fully developed ecotourism destination, Costa Rica provides a number of lessons to other states that have embarked on a similar path. Especially important is an examination of the 2008–2009 global recession on ecotourism in Costa Rica. As such, the first part of this chapter will address how the 2008–2009 global recession affected the Costa Rican ecotourism industry and what can be learned in the aftermath of a global economic downturn. This is important because many states throughout Latin America and the Caribbean have turned to tourism development in an attempt to diversify their export portfolios as a bulwark against external economic shocks. Like a lot of Latin American countries, Costa Rica has dealt with many economic crises throughout its history—many of which had profound effects on Costa Rican society and economy. In many ways the acceleration of the development of ecotourism in the late 1980s was born out of a number of economic crises during the so-called lost decade of the 1980s. In response to these crises, the Costa Rican government chose to employ a set of public policies that encouraged the growth and development of small-scale ecotourism enterprises and as a result the ecotourism industry in Costa Rica blossomed and local ownership proliferated. While many of the changes in the approach of the Costa Rican government to its tourism policies predate the 2008–2009 recession, the reaction of the Government of Costa Rica to the recession served to accelerate trends away from small-scale ecotourism and toward more traditional tourism forms such as large resorts and as a destination for cruise ship excursions.

The second part of this chapter discusses the lessons learned from examining the status of ecotourism in Costa Rica and the factors that helped to create the country's ecotourism industry. These factors include the need for an open economy and the ability to attract tourists as well as foreign direct investment. Also important are a regulatory and legal framework that encourages the growth of ecotourism related businesses, with a focus on small-scale operations which are much more likely to benefit local communities. Finally, since sustainable ecotourism takes place in the natural environment, policy makers should take measures to protect the environment so ecotourism can provide income to local communities over the long term. Utilizing the ideas inherent in sustainable ecotourism will be one of the key challenges for states after the recession and its effects on tourist arrivals.

THE IMPACT OF THE 2008–2009 GLOBAL RECESSION ON COSTA RICA

Given the centrality of ecotourism development to many states throughout Latin America and the Caribbean and the necessity of engaging with globalization via neoliberal free market reforms to grow the industry, it is important to assess the various ways in which the 2008–2009 global economic recession affected ecotourism. For many states, the recession caused a great deal of panic among policy makers as tourism arrivals and revenue plummeted. Given this downturn in tourism in addition to a variety of other economic problems throughout the region, it is important for states to remain attentive to the effects of policy changes that affect the natural environment and consequently the state's ability to benefit from ecotourism development in the long run. This is especially important given the frequency of economic crises throughout much of Latin America history.

Case in point is Costa Rica which until the 2008–2009 recession had enjoyed an almost unbroken string of successes in developing its ecotourism industry since its infancy in the mid-twentieth century and quickly rose to become the preeminent ecotourism destination in the world. Not surprisingly, the global economic crisis that began in December 2007 had a sharp short-term negative effect on global tourism flows and represented "the first serious downturn faced by the [tourism] sector at [the] global level." (UNWTO and ILO 2013, 6) In addition to being the first serious global level downturn in the tourism industry, the 2008–2009 global economic crisis also questioned the notion that the flow of tourists would never diminish as the period prior to the recession had been one of ever-increasing tourist arrivals worldwide. With the uncertainty of the global recession the late summer of 2008 was a particularly bad time for tourism as "world tourism activity started to slow significantly between June and August 2008, owing to the continuing deterioration in real incomes and consumer expectations, the volatility of exchange rates and the squeeze on consumer credit resulting from the financial crisis." (ECLAC 2008, 17)

Exacerbating these issues was the attitude among many Latin America policy makers at the time that their economies had matured to the point of immunity from economic problems in other parts of the world, particularly problems emanating from the United States. For instance, Brazilian President Luiz Inacio Lula da Silva famously stated "a few years ago, if the United States coughed, Brazil got pneumonia. Now we have diversified, we don't depend so much on one or two countries. . . . Ask [President] Bush about the crisis because it's his, not mine." (Kraul 2008) Given the interconnected nature of the globalized world economy, this view proved false because "a lot of what has helped Latin America's economies in recent years— access to capital markets, foreign investments, remittances from emigrants, the price of natural resources—depends on the health of the global marketplace. Any time the U.S. stock markets lose almost $7 trillion in a year—twice Latin America's gross domestic product, the ripple effects will be felt south of the Rio Grande." (Vargas-Llosa 2009, 21)

As the US economy slowed, both demand for Latin American imports to, as well as foreign direct investment from the United States to the region also slowed significantly. Further exacerbating this situation is that the United States is also the largest source of tourists for Costa Rica, contributing 39 percent of all tourist arrivals in 2008 and 2009. Not only were tourist numbers down overall, the ones who still traveled to Costa Rica in 2008 and 2009 spent less money as a 4.6 percent drop in tourist arrivals translated to a revenue decline of 8.3 percent. (*Instituto Costarricense de Turismo* 2011) Given the downturn in tourist arrivals, one of the biggest dangers of the recession is that it would motivate policy makers to put resources toward more traditional types of tourism and away from more environmentally sensitive forms. In an editorial in the January 2009 issue of the *Journal of Sustainable Tourism* coeditors Bill Bramwell and Bernard Lane warns that many policy makers will be tempted to do just that:

> The danger is that increasing proportions of tourism businesses and private and public sector organisations [*sic*] may decide they lack the resources to invest in the infrastructure, facilities and training needed for more sustainable products, and the ability to pay for environmental or social enhancements. Instead, they may focus on the short term considerations of reducing costs and securing immediate financial returns. Such responses could have highly damaging consequences for sustainability. (1)

What is interesting about the effects of the 2008–2009 global recession on tourism to Costa Rica is that while it dropped sharply in the summer of 2008, it rebounded very quickly with the number of arrivals and associated revenue quickly bouncing back. While the global economic crisis ushered in fifteen consecutive months of negative growth, it peaked in March 2009 when there was a 12 percent decrease in tourism arrivals around the world and despite this downturn, in 2010, the tourism sector rebounded faster than expected and fully compensated for the losses caused by the economic crisis at the global level, posting a growth rate of international tourist arrivals of 7 percent. (UNWTO and ILO 2013, 6) Part of the reason that tourist arrivals rebounded after the recession is in many places prices were adjusted down in an attempt to recoup as much of the losses as possible and to encourage people to travel. In fact, writing in early 2010, Ritchie, Amaya Molinar, and Frechtling found that "overall travel prices have fallen twice as fast in the current recession as they did after the 9/11 attacks." (13) As the data below indicates, the post-recession decline in tourism quickly bounced back and then surpassed pre-recession levels.

The recession also created uncertainty for Latin America in many other areas of the economy in addition to tourism as the recession represented an abrupt "cyclical downturn, mostly triggered by weaker exports, including for tourism, and less financial inflows. In addition, remittances, which are a

Table 1.1. Tourist Arrivals in Costa Rica: 2007–2013.

Year	*Tourist Arrivals*	*Tourism Income*	*Per Tourist Income*
2007	1,979,798	1,927,400,000	973
2008	2,089,174	2,174,100,000	1040
2009	1,922,579	1,805,800,000	939
2010	2,099,829	1,857,600,000	884
2011	2,192,059	1,988,400,000	907
2012	2,343,213	2,088,700,000	891
2013	2,427,941	2,253,300,000	928

In US Dollars.
Source: *Instituto Costarricense de Turismo* 2011 and 2013.

major source of income in many countries in the region, have slowed down, increasing pressures on reserves and threatening the availability of resources for credit growth." (Kandil 2009, 979) The 2008–2009 recession also made clear yet again those countries that have been unable to diversify their economies were hit the hardest. In the midst of the crisis, Alvaro Vargas-Llosa argued that "countries that are dependent on commodities are being severely affected (while) other nations whose exports have diversified . . . are being less hurt by the current environment or at least have more flexibility to respond." (2009, 21).

Given the panic caused by the recession among policy makers throughout the region, there was a lot of pressure for states to take action to remedy the situation. Similarly to the president of Brazil, Costa Rican President Óscar Arias was reticent to declare Costa Rica a victim of the global recession. However, after months of denying that the country was in the midst of a downturn, in January of 2009 President Arias outlined his plans for a stimulus package for Costa Rica in his *Plan Escudo* (Shield Plan) as a reaction to the recession. He also spoke bluntly regarding Costa Rica's predicament. "This international crisis will mean a strong economic contraction which will very probably be reflected in an increase in poverty and unemployment. There will also be less tourism and decreased exports and foreign direct investment." (Arias 2009) In the *Plan Escudo*, President Arias advances a proposal for economic recovery based on four pillars, each representing the government's "efforts to integrate the concerns of all." These four pillars included families, workers, businesses and the financial sector. The *Plan Escudo* was written as a comprehensive stimulus plan in the hopes of an economy-wide recovery and includes several measures to protect the most vulnerable of Costa Rica's citizens. Arias promised to increase in Social Security spending by 15 percent and provide services in nutrition and education on the weekends to children who attend a government-run Center for Education and Nutrition-Integrated Center for Child Health in the thirty-seven poorest cantons in the country. In addition the centers will send food home with the students for themselves and three family members. Arias also suggested an increase in school scholarship and various measures aimed at helping Costa Ricans struggling to stay in their homes including partial debt forgiveness and temporarily lowered interest rates on existing loans. In addition, the president asked companies to think about lowering the salaries of their highest paid employees and granted some labor flexibility to the tourism industry by annualizing work hours for employees so they could work less in the low season and more in the high season while adhering to Costa Rican wage laws. (Arias 2015)

While these measures had some positive effects on the Costa Rican economy, they also reflect the long term trend in Costa Rica to boost employment to the exclusion of other parts of the economy. As the IMF points out,

> The counter-cyclical budgetary stimulus imparted in 2009 pushed the deficit above 5 percent of GDP in 2010 (mainly through a rise in wages and transfers). The deficit has been creeping up further since then, placing the public debt-to-GDP ratio on an unsustainable upward trajectory, which is fast approaching levels shown to increase risks of disorderly adjustment for emerging economies. (International Monetary Fund 2015)

This desire for full employment is also what underlies the switch from small-scale ecotourism to a more traditional sun and surf tourism and an increase in the cruise traffic to Costa Rican ports.

The danger of economic policy that seeks to solve a temporary problem with a permanent solution is nothing new in Latin America and has often manifested itself as a move back to traditional exports and economic activities and away from more nontraditional sources of foreign exchange. In fact, writing about the 1973 OPEC embargo and its effects on Latin America James H. Street (1978) states that "an ironic effect of the recession was that it caused countries that had been developing nontraditional exports in order to reduce their dependence on primary commodities to fall back into the old pattern. Faced with a foreign exchange shortage, governments once more stimulated traditional exports." (71) Unfortunately, a short-term economic downtown created by the 2008–2009 global recession encouraged policy makers in Costa Rica to do just that.

COSTA RICA MOVES AWAY FROM ECOTOURISM

One of the most interesting parts of the development of ecotourism in Costa Rica is its transition from a place off the beaten track starting in the 1960s and 1970s to one of the most heavily visited small countries in the world by the 1990s. As ecotourism grew it tended to attract tourists that were older, better educated, willing to stay longer in-country, and spent more money while on a trip, with their top three reported activities as the desire for a wilderness setting, wildlife viewing, and hiking. (Epler Wood 2002, 21) However with the changes to ecotourism in Costa Rica over the last decade or so, the nature of tourists traveling there has also changed as there are fewer and fewer classic "ecotourists" and more and more sun-and-sand tourists as well as those who visit Costa Rica on a cruise. Brida and Zapata (2010) found that "Costa Rica's average cruise passenger is older, less educated and more American." (336) This is important because one of the key elements of Costa Rican ecotourism was its ability to draw ecotourists based on a specific set of needs that helped to create Costa Rica's small-scale ecotourism industry that was supportive of environmental sustainability and was better able to keep income from ecotourism activities in-country.

The erosion of Costa Rica's reputation as a small-scale and sustainable ecotourism destination is due to the coalescence of the downturn in tourist arrivals created by the 2008–2009 recession and paradoxically the oversaturation of the tourism industry which motivated the perceived need for new markets. Rather than continue to carve out a niche as an ecotourism destination, Costa Rican policy makers in recent years have attempted to appeal to a broader market by going mainstream. This change is in part due to the product life cycle for tourism first developed by Butler (1980) in which destinations are discovered, grow and develop, experience success, stagnate then either decline or rejuvenate and in part due to poor decisions by Costa Rican policy makers who shifted focus away from ecotourism development projects in a misguided attempt to create new markets.

While tourist preferences vary over time, this change from ecotourism to more traditional resort and cruise tourism is a major shift in Costa Rica's focus as a tourism destination. These changes have their roots in ecotourism policies in Costa Rica going back to the mid-1990s, but have accelerated due to the impacts of the 2008–2009 global recession and appear to be accelerating further. One of the most important areas of change in Costa Rican tourism is the development of large-scale resorts, particularly on the Pacific coast. Chief among these is the Papagayo Project in the Guanacaste province of northwest Costa Rica which broke ground in 1995 at a cost of US$3 billion and has been dubbed "Costa Rica's Cancún." This project was originally slated to have somewhere in the range of 25,000 to 30,000 hotel rooms—a number that is twice as much hotel capacity as the rest of the country combined. (Honey 2008, 165) Since that time the project has been somewhat scaled back, but still represents a massive alteration from traditional ecotourism in Costa Rica.

One of the major motivations for this project was the Costa Rican government's focus on economic policies that encourage employment and the government hoped that projects such as this would be able to create a large number of jobs at the resort in addition to associated industries such as construction. For the most part however, these projects have not led to the sort of large-scale employment desired by the government and Honey, Vargas, and Durham found that "despite projections that the [Papagayo Project] would generate employment for tens of thousands of local people, by 2008, the facilities in operation were recorded as producing only about 1400 jobs." (2010, 8) In addition to a very sparse record on job creation, these large-scale resort projects often have a negative effect on the environment. For instance, down the coast in Tamarindo, the area has lost approximately one half of its monkey population because developers destroyed their habitat and light pollution has contributed to a decline in the survival rate of leatherback turtle hatchings as the light disorients them, making it difficult for the turtles to reach the relative safety of the ocean. (McPhaul 2008)

In addition to the construction of large-scale resorts on the coast, the Costa Rican government has also pursued policies to increase the number of cruise ships to Costa Rican ports, also on the Pacific coast. Costa Rica has long been a port of call for cruise ships on its Caribbean coast, but only recently has planned to expand large-scale cruise tourism to both coasts in an attempt to boost cruise ship arrivals. Increasing cruise facilities is also attractive because once built the cruise lines contracted to use Costa Rican ports will do the majority of the work in bringing new tourists to Costa Rica as the cruise line will simply add the port of call to an existing route.

The vast majority of income from cruise passengers visiting Costa Rica, which is not very high to begin with, is also subject to a great deal of economic leakage as the cruise lines are based outside of Costa Rica and the excursions are paid for on the ship with only a fraction going to those who actually operate the tour. For instance, businesses in Puntarenas, on the Pacific side of Costa Rica "benefit little from cruise passenger arrivals since the vast majority immediately board buses to go on tours they have purchased onboard. These tours are run by a small number of large San José–based tour operators, with the cruise lines receiving a large percentage of fees." (57) These large cruise ship–based tour groups also serve as an impediment for overnight guests, who by and large will spend more than the cruise excursionists. A further issue is the use of cargo ports for cruise ships that often damage the facility and leave little additional income in the local community. For instance, "Caldera, a busy commercial port specially designed for cargo use, is also used for cruise ships, including as a 'home port' (where tours start and finish) for some small luxury cruises. Caldera has no local town or attractions within walking distance of the berths, other than a few local vendors selling handicrafts and coffee. Tourist passengers either leave immediately for Puntarenas or get on buses to go on packaged tours." (57)

Not only is the expansion of cruise tourism counter to Costa Rica's image as an environmentally sensitive ecotourism destination, but as these examples indicate, cruise ship tourism provides very little economic benefit for a destination country. This argument is verified by Brida and Zapata (2010) who concluded that "cruise activity does not have a significant economic impact on Costa Rica. Cruise tourism is a small (but increasing) importance in Costa Rica representing less than 2 percent of the expenditures of land tourism." (336) This finding is similar to Honey, Vargas, and Durham (2010) who in a study of tourism development on Costa Rica's Pacific coast concluded that:

> Large cruise tourism in Puntarenas and Caldera is not providing sufficient benefits to these urban areas or to the country as a whole to warrant pursuing a range of expansion plans under consideration. Plans to create a "home port"

> for large cruise lines and to build new cruise ship ports-of-call elsewhere along the coast or on offshore islands should be abandoned. (92)

Despite the scant evidence that cruise tourism positively contributes to neither the economy nor the natural environment of Costa Rica, Costa Rican tourism minister Wilhelm von Breymann stated in 2014 that "since the beginning of this administration, we have visualized cruise tourism as a spearhead for tourism growth, the generation of productive chains which benefit coastal communities and the positioning of our image as a distinct destination, suitable for development of tourism activities." (Central America Data)

While the difficulties faced by small economies like Costa Rica that need to balance economic development and employment with environmental preservation is nothing new, what makes Costa Rica unique is the move away from established standards of environmentally-based ecotourism toward forms of mass tourism that they had long rejected. Because of the changes in the approach to the tourism industry, the Costa Rican Hotel and Resorts Association has warned that "Costa Rica can no longer project the pure image of an eco-tourism paradise since reality shows investors are free to develop more and more projects without clear rules." (McPhaul 2008) One of the most important decisions for the Costa Rican government is whether they want to return to a tourism model based on ecotourism or if they want to create a tourism industry that has more in common with Cancún. As such, the future of Costa Rican ecotourism is not set in stone, but rather is based on the decision-making processes of Costa Rican politicians.

The Costa Rican case illustrates the need for good policy making within the context of neoliberalism in order to create ecotourism that is sustainable over the long term. Much of the success of Costa Rican ecotourism is attributable to policy choices over several decades that helped to create a comparative advantage in ecotourism, a comparative advantage that has eroded as Costa Rican politicians have begun to focus their efforts on other segments of the tourism industry. This tension between small-scale ecotourism and large-scale resort and cruise ship tourism is not inherent to neoliberalism, but instead is the intentional choice of politicians. Due to this, the Costa Rican case provides both an incentive for policy makers to engage in small-scale ecotourism development based on Costa Rica's success, but in many ways is also a cautionary tale for states to remain faithful to ecotourism development plans centered on engaging the outside world while also providing a uniquely small-scale ecotourism experience. A turn to large resorts and cruise tourism is not the inevitable slippery slope of neoliberalism, but is the byproduct of poor government decision making.

WHAT CAN BE LEARNED FROM COSTA RICA?

Given the amount of time that Costa Rica has spent as the preeminent ecotourism destination in the world, what can other states learn from the Costa Rican model of development including its successes as well as it missteps? Furthermore, in what ways have they been able to successfully pair ecotourism with policies that help to attract foreign direct investment? One of the most successful aspects of Costa Rican ecotourism is that they were able to build ecotourism, particularly in the early days of the industry, around the creation of small-scale business in which most of the income generated stayed in the local community. As Honey, Vargas, and Durham (2010) point out "over the last two decades, Costa Rica has earned an international reputation as a leader in high value, small-scale, nature based tourism or ecotourism and, more broadly, as a leader in environmentalism." (13)

The Costa Rican model of development is based on three primary factors: ecotourism development, the attraction of foreign direct investment and the export of high value agricultural goods such as coffee. One of the most important facets of the Costa Rican economy over the last few decades is the move away from a dependence on agricultural export toward and economy based on the development of ecotourism and the attraction of foreign direct investment, particularly in high technology manufacturing. What made the convergence of FDI and ecotourism successful was the manner in which economic policies in each area are mutually reinforcing and Costa Rica was able to grow its economy over the last several decades by pursuing policies based on the intersection between foreign direct investment and ecotourism development. Therefore, these policy intersections are the key to understanding economic development in Costa Rica as they both encourage outside investment as well as development of an ecotourism industry.

Not only is sustainable ecotourism a better choice for environmental protection, but there is also some evidence that ecotourists are less likely to be affected by a recession due to having above average income and a unique outlook on travel. For instance, in a study conducted at the height of the recession in 2009, 75 percent of responsible travelers reported that the credit crunch would not change their travel plans. (Gray 2009, 7) This also means that operators who provide tourism services for ecotourists also often fare better in an economic downturn. Honey, Vargas, and Durham (2010) found that

> the impacts of the current economic recession on Costa Rica's tourism industry appear to indicate that the nature-based tourism accommodations, tour operators, and activities have fared better than the coastal resort market. The reasons appear to be several: that ecotourists, even those who seek luxury along with nature, are more experienced travelers who place high value on

quality travel and are likely to continue to travel even in tough economic times. (71)

With the ability of tourism to quickly bounce back after an economic downturn, it is important for states to continue building an ecologically-based tourism industry regardless of any temporary economic downturns. One of the most important lessons from Costa Rica is that the ecotourism industry will quickly bounce back and not to alter the long-term strategy of sustainable ecotourism based on short-term economic problems. This is especially important in smaller economies such as Belize, Nicaragua, and Panama which have searched for most of their histories for nontraditional exports they can use for a comparative advantage. In addition, individual tourism businesses are better able to react to price signals caused by external economic factors and alter their cost structures accordingly. The ability of individual businesses to react to an external shock by lowering prices to attract ecotourists is also an important reason that ecotourism can bounce back quickly from a downturn.

Another strategy used by Costa Rica as it was developing an ecotourism industry was to focus not only on the international market, but also to appeal to its domestic tourist market. This early development of the domestic market, starting after World War II, gave Costa Rica a basic tourist infrastructure

Table 1.2. Intersections between foreign direct investment and ecotourism development policies.

Policy intersection between ecotourism development and the attraction of foreign direct investment:	*Attracts foreign direct investment and builds ecotourism via:*
1. Regime type and rule of law.	Building a democratic regime in which there is respect for the rule of law, that in turn improves the social stability desired by both investors as well as ecotourists.
2. Development of human capital.	An educated populace that is able to serve the needs of businesses that wish to operate in-country and ecotourists that wish to visit.
3. Development and maintenance of infrastructure.	An infrastructure that can adequately serve the needs of all those doing business in or visiting Costa Rica.
4. Economic liberalization	Integration into the world economy, facilitating the ease of financial transactions for both investors and tourists
5. Environmental protection.	Environmental protection that protects the things that ecotourists visit Costa Rica to see.

as they later began to attract international visitors. In addition, as international tourists spent less money during the recession, the expenditures of Costa Ricans traveling in their own country actually went up. This led to an advertising campaign focused on the domestic market named "*Vamos a Turistear*" (let's take a trip) which further resulted in approximately 700 direct bookings and 100,000 visits to lodges, restaurants, theme parks, and other tourism destinations. (Lopez) In this way, domestic tourists can provide a bulwark against economic downturns and often provide a steadier source of income for ecotourism businesses.

With tourism initially created for the domestic market of a developing country, for much of Costa Rica's time as an ecotourism destination its primary competitive advantages have been price, value and its unique ecological features. Given its variety of climates, beaches, volcanos, and tropical environs, Costa Rica provided an excellent value for travelers that would have otherwise stayed home or paid a much more significant amount of money to travel elsewhere. The perceived value of a Costa Rican vacation was further enhanced for North American visitors by its proximity to the United States and Canada which represents the clear majority of its visitors.

When visiting Costa Rica, a common refrain among many tourists is that the country is more expensive than the thought it would be. This opinion was validated by the World Economic Forum who found that Costa Rica was the most expensive destination in Central America, ranking slightly less expensive than the United States for tourists. (World Economic Forum) A lot of the increased cost for tourists comes from the increasing cost of doing business in Costa Rica which is then passed along to visitors. In particular, utility rates for things like phone service and electricity tend to be expensive as well as gasoline. Another part of the problem is that increased prices are also due in part to the attitude among many Costa Ricans that ecotourists, particularly those from the United States, are an endless source of revenue that will pay any price since they are on vacation. Given that one of Costa Rica's comparative advantages has long been price, as prices increase this could very easily push visitors to new and less expensive options. As the *Boston Globe* states in a December 2014 article about the best places to travel in 2015, "forget Costa Rica—old news. Industry experts are calling Nicaragua the hottest destination in Central America, and one of its best bargains." (Bair 2014) Given the centrality of price and value to a large segment of visitors, it is imperative for states that want to grow an ecotourism industry to create a business environment in which costs are kept as low as possible. The US State Department (2015) reports that the "challenges to the country's competitiveness, including rising operating costs, a complicated legal environment, excessive bureaucratic red tape, and infrastructure deficiencies, are fueling caution on the part of investors." (3)

Traditionally, one of Costa Rica's most important attributes for attracting tourists as well as investors is its long-term political, social, economic stability and rule of law. Many of the factors that led to a stable Costa Rica are based on its unique history that served to set it apart from its neighbors, however there are still many things for other states to learn. First and foremost, states that want to create an environment that is attractive to tourists as well as investors need to make a long-term commitment to democracy and the rule of law. While the business environment in Costa Rica is not perfect and there are some problems with the court system and the bureaucracy, which is all too often inefficient, the general atmosphere for business and investment is very good and outside investment is actively sought.

Part of the dividend created by a stable political, social and economic system is the ability to better develop human capital, which is vital to building a successful ecotourism industry. Costa Rica has done a particularly good job in training people for tourism and tourism related jobs and the creation of an educated workforce is one of Costa Rica's biggest comparative advantages. "Thanks to past investment policies in education, Costa Rica's adult literacy rate is close to 100 percent, and primary school enrollment is nearly universal. A considerable number of people have some knowledge of English, a result of the introduction of foreign language instruction in primary schools in 1994 and the prevalence of English-speaking tourists." (Cordero and Paus 2008, 5) While it is somewhat cliché to state the importance of education to national development, Costa Rica has been able to embark on a targeted education strategy in which preference is given to high technology education, English instruction and hospitality related courses of instruction. These areas were selected due to their compatibility with economic development based on sustainable ecotourism and foreign direct investment. As such, other states should similarly target their educational system to their own unique comparative advantages. Costa Rica has done a particularly good job in training its ecotourism tour guides so they are better able to enhance the educational aspects of a tour for visitors. One of the earliest of these programs trained tour guides in Tortuguero, a very popular sea turtle nesting site, to be cognizant of the needs of wildlife, what a tour guide needs to know about the area, what tourists find interesting and the economic feasibility of tourism operations. (Jacobson and Robles 1992, 702) These programs help to enhance the experience of ecotourists and help to ensure return visits and a broader understanding and appreciation of environmental issues.

The Costa Rican case also illustrates the necessity of building an infrastructure that will help to enhance its ability to attract tourists and investors. In Costa Rica, infrastructure tends to be better in tourist zones as well as in established free trade zones created to attract foreign direct investment than it is in other parts of the country. For many years, Costa Rican infrastructure was the envy of the region, however, in recent years, many aspects of its infrastructure have started to need upgrade or replacement. The US State Department declares that "much of Costa Rica's basic infrastructure—ports, roads, water systems—needs major upgrading," (3) which is an impediment to the economy. There have been some notable improvements such as the upgrade at Daniel Oduber Quiros Airport in Liberia, Guanacaste, to modernize and increase the number of flights in and out of northwestern Costa Rica. In addition, Costa Rica has secured a US$450 million loan from the Inter-American Development Bank to improve its infrastructure and has several goals:

> The project will repair or pave up to 110 kilometers of the national road network, widen 51 kilometers of roads from two to four lanes, and build or repair 19 bridges and nearly 400 meters of breakwater in ports. These measures are expected to help reduce vehicle operations by 7 percent and travel time by 28 percent. In addition, the improvements to roads and bridges are expected to help communities throughout the country to transport their products at lower cost and more efficiently to domestic and foreign markets. Better transformation infrastructure also will help Costa Ricans access social services by allowing them to reach health, education and other government facilities more easily and in timely fashion. (Inter-American Development Bank 2015)

With these improvements, Costa Rican infrastructure should be considerably better in the future. For too long the country's infrastructure, particularly its roads, have become an almost comical rite of passage for visiting tourists, for instance the road to Arenal volcano from La Fortuna, which had long been an interesting trek.

In an attempt to build a larger industrial base, especially in high-tech manufacturing, Costa Rica has also aggressively sought out foreign direct investment for many years. As such, the investment climate has been generally favorable and foreign direct investment is high and has been a significant contributor to economic growth. Since 2000, investment from Costa Rica has steadily risen and reached a high of over $2.6 billion in 2013 before dropping back to $2.1 billion in 2014. (US Department of State 2015, 3). As the primary promoter of investment in Costa Rica the Costa Rican Investment Promotion Agency (CINDE), has a number of incentive programs to entice high-tech companies to invest in the country. "The vast majority of these companies establish themselves in Free Trade Zones that enjoy certain fiscal benefits. Consistent with this orientation, the Costa Rican government was aggressive in signing free trade agreements, tax information agreements and generally participating in the global arena." (US Department of State 2015, 3) Many of the attributes discussed in this chapter are used as the major enticements for foreign direct investment into Costa Rica, including long-term stability, incentives for investors, as well as its close proximity to the United States. CINDE offers a 100 percent tax exemption with no expiration date for import/export customs duties, withholding tax on royalties, fees, dividends and interest income, sales tax on local purchases and stamp duty. They further provide an eight-year exemption for income taxes, followed by a further four-year period of a 50 percent tax exemption if the operation moves to San José. Outside of San José, the income tax period is twelve years of no taxes and six years of the 50 percent exemption. (CINDE) This further enhancement for investment outside the capital is due to the relatively uneven industrial development common throughout Central America and is a great strategy to induce investment outside of large metropolitan areas.

Although Costa Rica has created a favorable atmosphere for foreign direct investment, that does not mean that there are not occasionally setbacks-the biggest of which is the decision by microchip maker Intel to close its facility in the San José suburb of Alajuela which had been one of Costa Rica's biggest investment success stories. Although the exact reasons behind the closure are unclear, the move appears to have more to do with Intel's attempts to streamline its manufacturing processes due to the shrinking personal computer market than any issues with Costa Rica's business environment. (Randewich 2015) That is not to say that the closing of the Intel plant is not a blow to Costa Rica as it was a source of pride among many Costa Ricans and provided approximately 25 percent of the country's exports.

Costa Rica also demonstrates the necessity of strong environmental protection so that an ecotourism industry can flourish. Costa Rica also benefitted from the emergence of the environmental movement before the development of either an ecotourism industry or a large manufacturing base. This allowed for the advent of environmental protection prior to the needs of either industry and gave the environment a much more effective voice as a large chunk of the Costa Rican workforce made its living off of the natural environment via ecotourism. The development of environmental protection policies prior to the development of large-scale industries is very important in ensuring that ecotourism sites are preserved for future use. This is especially important given that so much of what makes Costa Rica a popular destination is its world-class national park system, which is protected by the Costa Rican government. Currently, almost 27 percent of Costa Rican land is protected as a national park. (World Bank)

Managing Costa Rica's tourism industry is the *Instituto Costarricense de Turismo* (ICT) which since its founding in 1955 has directed nearly every aspect of Costa Rican tourism. This includes the promotion of activities—both to tourists and investors—tourism planning, and the development of quality control systems such as ecotourism certification. (*Instituto Costarricense de Turismo*) Since Costa Rica gets the majority of its tourists from the United States, advertising efforts have long been focused there and are an important part of the ICT's job. This includes the latest advertising campaign called "Save the Americans: Costa Rican Animals for Overworked

Americans," and features many of Costa Rica's most well-known animals imploring overworked Americans to visit. (*Instituto Costarricense de Turismo*) Previous advertising campaigns, particularly the previous ICT slogan "No Artificial Ingredients" have used Costa Rica's environmentally-conscious image as a selling point. Costa Rican tourism has benefitted greatly from the work of the ICT and states that wish to improve their tourism industry should look to the organization as a model. In particular is the ICT's management of the Certificate for Sustainable Tourism which monitors the environmental sustainability practices of the industry. In addition, an effective tourism bureau can help to plan and manage tourism so that it does not happen in a haphazard way. Given these lessons, both positive and negative, other states are better able to embark upon sustainable ecotourism as a development strategy and benefit from increased foreign direct investment based on the ways in which the interests of each intersect. In addition, many of these reforms are more easily accomplished because of the globalized world in which competition knows no national borders.

CASE SELECTION

In a review of papers published in the *Journal of Sustainable Tourism*, Lu and Nepal found that research in ecotourism had "shortcomings in need of attention [including] research in developing countries, especially in Africa and Central and South America [which are] still poorly represented." (2009, 14) A major motivation for this book is to analyze the state of ecotourism development in countries that have often been overlooked by scholars—while a fair amount of work has been done on Belize, very little work has been done to analyze the viability of Nicaragua or Panama at developing a sustainable ecotourism industry that can improve people's lives while also preserving the environment. Another major factor for this book and in the selection of cases is to examine three countries that have many similarities to Costa Rica and for which the Costa Rican model of development could be a success.

The three cases in this book were each selected for very specific reasons. Belize was selected because it represents the main competitor for Costa Rica not only in Central America, but in all of Latin America. The ability of the Belizeans to either copy what Costa Rica has done or in some instances make a different set of decisions, will speak volumes to the future of sustainable ecotourism in the country. The lessons of Costa Rica have a unique opportunity to be employed in Belize to the extent that it is possible that they could become the top destination in the region. Panama was selected because they have a somewhat developed (eco)tourism industry based around the Canal, but also have a lot of potential for ecotourism. Similarly to the situation in

Belize, Panama could apply many of the lessons from Costa Rica, with much more room for growth. Finally, Nicaragua was selected because it is a destination that has a lot of room to grow and develop and has never really been considered a vacation destination due to its history of conflict—something that is rapidly changing as Nicaragua is becoming one of the world's new ecotourism "hot spots."

Chapter Two

Nicaragua: Ecotourism in the Land of Nicas?

Nicaragua has one of the most interesting, and turbulent, histories of any country in Central America and it has often been central to the struggle between rival powers. Since its conquest by Spain, Nicaragua has endured civil wars, outside interventions, and long periods of social unrest. As Richard L. Millett (1988) puts it "Nicaragua's history is largely the history of disruptions—by foreigners, by its own leaders (or would-be leaders) and even by the forces of nature: earthquakes, volcanic eruptions, hurricanes." (98) For many potential tourists, Nicaragua is still remembered as a place of violent conflict where the US-backed *contra* rebels battled the Sandinista government for over a decade. Memories of the conflict are beginning to fade, however, and foreigners (particularly Americans) are starting to see Nicaragua as "Costa Rica 30 years ago"—beautiful beaches, cheap prices (including real estate) and an exotic locale. Similarly to Costa Rica, Nicaragua boasts many interesting natural attractions such as rainforests, flora and fauna, and volcanoes. One key difference from Costa Rica is the much larger array of cultural attractions such as churches and other architecture in a much more attractive city environment in places like Granada, Masaya, and León. Due to these factors, over the last decade or so, Nicaragua has become one of ecotourism's new hot spots, replacing Costa Rica as an ecotourism destination for a more adventurous brand of ecotourist who now view Costa Rica as being on the beaten path. Given the changes in Nicaragua, what are the chances that it can parlay its natural capital into an effective system of sustainable ecotourism that is able to contribute to economic development and environmental preservation while also attracting foreign direct investment?

PRECOLONIAL NICARAGUA

Discovered by Christopher Columbus on his fourth journey to the New World, the conquest and colonization of Nicaragua was an extension of Spain's ongoing colonization of Panama with Spain able to assert control over what would become Nicaragua in 1524. (Walker and Wade 2011, 8) When the Spaniards arrived in Nicaragua they found two distinct ethnic groups: the Indian population in western Nicaragua, which was more closely related to the Aztec and Mayan populations and the peoples of eastern Nicaragua that had migrated from what is now Colombia. (Library of Congress 2014) After the Spaniards conquered (or mostly conquered) the country they settled, for the most part, in the western part of the country as they did throughout their colonies in Central America. To this day, approximately 90 percent of Nicaraguans live on the Pacific side of the country.

As the Spaniards conquered and settled the western part of Nicaragua, they set out to conquer Indian groups that had long been in conflict with each other. The long history of animosity and conflict among these groups helped to make conquest possible, despite Spain's huge numerical disadvantage. The Spaniards were able to exploit the traditional rivalries among groups that were eager to enlist the Spaniards to help them to defeat their rivals. Walker and Wade (2011) argue that in pre-Columbian Nicaragua "warfare, slavery, and involuntary tribute by the weak to the strong were among the basic ingredients of pre-Columbian life in the west." (8) The existence of these exploitative social systems was the key to the Spaniard's ability to colonize large swaths of Latin America and bring it under their control.

SPANISH COLONIALISM IN NICARAGUA

Due to the political and social structures of pre-Columbian Nicaragua, the Spaniards had a relatively easy time grafting their own forms of slavery and exploitation onto the existing systems after they had completed their conquest. In fact, Walker and Wade (2011) argue that "many of the traits that characterized colonial rule existed long before the first conquistadores set foot on the land." (8) In addition, the relatively unsettled land also lacked the social, political, and economic organization to withstand the colonization of the Spaniards. One of the long lasting legacies of the precolonial period is that modern Nicaragua derives its name from Nicarao, a prominent indigenous leader from that period.

Like elsewhere in the New World, Spain wanted to colonize Central America in order to become rich and convert souls to the Catholic faith. When the Spaniards arrived in Nicaragua, they found a fairly large native population along with a fair amount of gold and silver. These riches proved to be short-lived and when Nicaragua's gold and silver deposits ran out the Spaniards shipped almost 200,000 Indians to Panama as slave labor. (Millet 1988, 100) Due to this, Nicaragua went from a place that Spaniards thought could be a very wealthy colony, to a backwater attached to the Audencia of Guatemala, along with most of Central America. These early years of colonialism would help to make Nicaragua, and Central America generally, peripheral to the Spanish Crown, as such:

> The authority emanating from Guatemala City was weak at best, and political control in the region decentralized around the provincial towns. The weakness of central authority in part reflected the wretched state of communications in the isthmus, but the lack of roads and administrative infrastructure themselves resulted from Central America's limited economic importance to the Spanish crown. During the colonial period, Central America generated few exports compared to other Spanish possessions in the New World. (Weeks 1986, 33)

The quick transformation from prominence to secondary status (at best) among Spanish colonies meant that "the early years of the colonial period had a lasting impact on the nature of Nicaraguan society and politics." (Walker and Wade 2011, 8) Similarly to other parts of Latin America, the most devastating impact of Spanish colonialism on Nicaragua was demographic, with a steep decline in the native population due in large part to warfare, new diseases, and slavery. In the first twenty years of colonization by the Spaniards, the native population in Nicaragua went from several hundred thousand to 1,548 a census that showed just 11,137 Indians in Nicaragua (Millet 1988, 100) Since Nicaragua did not appear to the Spaniards to provide much possibility of riches, they made very little investment in the country and began to concentrate their efforts toward proselytization of the native population. In addition, the lack of attention from the Spanish Crown also allowed rivalries within Nicaragua to fester unchecked.

> The Spanish built churches and monasteries, but few roads or schools. What they gave, besides their Mediterranean-style architecture, their language, plantation farming and Catholicism . . . was a rivalry between two groups: Conservatives, mostly aristocratic landowners, with close ties to Spain and the Church; and Liberals, generally native-born creoles, anticlerical and restive about Spanish rule. (100)

INDEPENDENCE AND POSTCOLONIAL NICARAGUA

Nicaragua, like its Central American neighbors, became independent from Spain in 1822 as a part of Mexico, then joined the Central American Federal Republic (CAF) in 1823 and finally became an independent state in 1838. The political climate in the decades after independence represented a number of political cleavages including the traditional rivalries between *peninsulares* and *criollos*, conservatives and liberals, and most importantly for post-independence Nicaragua, the cities of Granada and León. Granada was the center of the conservative faction which was made up in large part of traditional elite families and *peninsulares* that had held power during colonialism and who therefore wished to keep much of the colonial structure intact, including the power of the Catholic Church. León on the other hand was the center of the liberal faction, which were anticlerical, anti-Spain, and made up mostly of *criollos*. The rivalry between León and Granada was so paralyzing to the political development of Nicaragua that the country "had no national government as such until the presidency of José Santos Zelaya (1893–1909)." (Weeks 1986, 34)

The late nineteenth century would also see the rise of a coffee elite and consequent set of societal relations that would be a factor in the Sandinista revolution almost a hundred years later. President José Santos Zelaya had a particularly strong effect on the concentration of land into the hands of coffee farmers via his consolidation of the liberal agenda when he became president of Nicaragua via a coup d'état in 1893. Although the coffee business arrived late to Nicaragua compared to other Central American states, there was still a very large concentration of land to a very small number of coffee growers. For instance, "fifty percent of all land sales under Zelaya went to only 30 families, all of them Liberals. In 1900 just 57 growers received the bulk of government agricultural premiums paid in that year." (Paige 1997, 157)

Zelaya's policies not only concentrated wealth into the hands of a relative few, it also alienated workers via a system of forced labor that would have a strong effect on societal relations for most of the twentieth century. Making matters worse, while workers made very little money and struggled to pay their bills, the coffee elite's profits grew as the popularity of coffee expanded. Part of the reason that income derived from the coffee trade expanded under Zelaya is that the system of large landed estates created by Zelaya's policies helped to double the amount of coffee exported under the Zelaya Administration. (157) The dominance of coffee growers and the large concentration of wealth meant that virtually every elite family in Nicaragua had some connection to the production of coffee. Given the thrust of Zelaya's policies and the power of the coffee elite, it is not surprising that "[Zelaya's] liberal reforms created the pattern of monocultural agro-export production by large landed estates dependent on impoverished wage laborers that was a characteristic feature of twentieth-century Nicaraguan agriculture and a principal cause of the Sandinista revolution in 1979." (157–8)

The administration of Zelaya would also usher in a long period of direct interference in Nicaraguan politics by the United States, who was upset with Zelaya's reticence to allow the Americans to build a canal across Nicaragua to connect the Pacific and Atlantic oceans. Although the United States would ultimately help to engineer Zelaya's ouster by sending troops to Bluefields after stating that they would support a conservative overthrow of the liberal Zelaya, the Canal was built in Panama and Nicaragua would be governed by a pro-US puppet regime supported by Nicaraguan conservatives. (Walker and Wade 2011, 17) This regime also quickly collapsed and brought about the invasion of US troops to make certain that US interests were protected. The invasion would morph into a US occupation of Nicaragua that lasted from 1912 to 1925, with a second occupation from 1926 to 1933. (18) This second US occupation of Nicaragua helped to produce the two main figures whose legacies would dominate the remainder of twentieth-century Nicaragua, Augusto Sandino and Anastasio Somoza García.

Augusto Sandino, who would ruthlessly battle US troops during the occupation and then with Somoza's National troops when the Americans left, was the prime architect of Nicaraguan nationalism. Although he would later give his name to the Sandinistas, Sandino himself was no socialist in any real sense. "Although Sandino at times described himself as a 'socialist' dedicated to a coming 'proletariat explosion' . . . there is no evidence that he ever developed any systematic class-based ideology of any socio-economic program beyond anti-Yankee nationalism." (Paige 1997, 171) As such, Sandino's concerns centered on Nicaragua and forcing the retreat of American forces. For his part, Anastasio Somoza Garcia took control of military when the United States left in 1933 and took up the American's war against Sandino and then installed himself as president in 1937 initiating a family dynasty that would dominate Nicaraguan politics until 1979. After an intense rivalry between the two men, Sandino was killed by Somoza's troops in 1934, however his name would give rise to the modern Sandinista Party decades later. The rivalry between the Somoza family and their supporters and the Sandinistas would become the crux of Nicaraguan politics for the rest of the twentieth century.

THE SANDINISTA REVOLUTION AND THE CIVIL WAR OF THE 1980s

For many Americans, the civil war in Nicaragua is a well-known Cold War hot spot in which US-backed *contra* rebels fought against Soviet and Cuban-backed Sandinista communists. According to Jeffery M. Paige (1997), rather than conceptualizing the civil wars of Central America as just another Cold War conflict between superpowers, Central American civil wars of the 1980s, including the conflict in Nicaragua, should be seen as deeply rooted in the social and economic structures of the region. (3) The roots of the conflict can be traced back to the colonial period which imparted to Nicaragua an uneven system of development that created a very small, ultra-wealthy elite and a very large population of people who lived in extreme poverty. However the direct cause of the Nicaraguan revolution and subsequent civil war is the US occupation and the rise of Sandino, which helped to develop what Robert L. Millet calls the "tradition of rebellion." (1988, 98) For the better part of the twentieth century, the Somoza family and their associates helped to foster this tradition of rebellion by governing Nicaragua as their personal fiefdom which they would defend at any cost. As Anastasio Somoza famously said "they will have to kill me first. I shall never quit power like Fulgencio Batista in Cuba or Pérez Jiménéz in Venezuela. I'll only leave like Rafael Leonidas Trujillo of the Dominican Republic, that is dead." (Walker and Wade 2011, 36)

Although twentieth-century Nicaragua is marked by rebellions, first against the US occupation, then against the United States, the unraveling of the Somoza regime began in earnest with his reaction to the 1972 earthquake in Managua and the subsequent rebuilding efforts which the regime used to line their own pockets rather than rebuild the country. (31) Long unhappy with the Somozas, the combination of poverty and the destruction of a large swath of Managua served to focus the efforts of antiregime elements who stepped up their small-scale attacks. The ever-increasing unhappiness of average Nicaraguans, coupled with Somoza's intransience meant the ensuing conflict would take a heavy toll on Nicaragua. In July of 1979, the Sandinistas finally overthrew Somoza, who fled and was eventually killed in Paraguay in 1981. Despite the unsavory nature of Somoza, the Sandinista revolution was instantly controversial both inside and outside Nicaragua and would draw the immediate attention of the United States, which was fearful of a communist victory in its own backyard. Prior to the Sandinista victory in 1979 the Carter Administration had indicated that the United States would not be involved in the dispute in Nicaragua including a statement by Secretary of State Cyrus Vance in mid-February 1978 that the US Embassy in Managua should "make clear to the Nicaraguans that this is of a purely Nicaraguan internal political character and one which the US will play no role." (Schmidli 2012, 70) Due to this type of rhetoric from the Carter Administration in the time directly before and after the Sandinistas took power, there was hope in Nicaragua that the United States would not intervene in the revolution. Not only did it appear as though the Carter Administration would stay on the sidelines during any conflict in Nicaragua at the very beginning the Sandinista government enjoyed some reluctant acceptance from President Carter's Administration including $100 million in foreign aid in an attempt to upgrade the United States' profile in postrevolutionary societies and hopefully play a role in the reconstruction efforts. (Vilas 2004, 50)

Despite its desire to stay out of the conflict in Nicaragua, the Carter Administration started to change its mind on the role of the United States in Nicaragua after the Sandinista victory and subsequently cut aid to Nicaragua when it was discovered that the Sandinista government had signed a trade and cooperation agreement with the Soviet Union. (51) Despite early hopes that the Carter Administration would create a new approach to US Policy in Central America, Nicaragua quickly became a Cold War hot spot in the eyes of Washington.

> As thousands of Nicaraguans celebrated the Sandinistas' revolutionary triumph in Managua's main square on 9 July 1979, the Carter Administration was transitioning to a more traditional Cold War posture. In the face of Third World upheaval and perceived resurgence of Soviet adventurism during his final two years in the Oval Office, Carter tacked an increasingly hawkish course—shifting human rights, multilateralism, and non-intervention increasingly to the back burner as policy priorities and establishing the framework for the subsequent Reagan Administration's aggressive pursuit of containment in the Third World. (Schmidli 2012, 82–83)

Although President Carter would begin the shift in US policy toward Nicaragua, it was the Reagan Administration that would aggressively attempt to bring down the Sandinista regime by implementing policies that would make governing Nicaragua very difficult for the regime, not least arming and funding the *contras* in their counterrevolution against the regime. While Nicaraguans saw their struggles against the Somoza dynasty in terms of their own poverty and the opulence of the Somozas as well as other elites, the Reagan Administration conceived of the civil war in Nicaraguan purely in Cold War terms. "[Reagan's] rationale for supporting the contras was to impose foreign policy restraint on the Sandinistas in the interest of regional security: to interdict arms supplies to the leftist guerillas in El Salvador, to check the Sandinista military build-up, [and] to prevent a Soviet-Cuban beachhead." (Jentleson 1991, 66)

Throughout the 1980s, the Reagan Administration stepped up its efforts to remove to the Sandinistas from power through directly funding the *contras*, to isolating the Sandinista regime economically and politically. With the 1990 election of Violeta Chamorro, the rejection of the Sandinistas was complete (for the moment). The election of Chamorro however should not necessarily be seen as a victory for the *contras* or the Reagan Administration's policies in Nicaragua. For many Nicaraguans, Chamorro represented a "middle ground" between the old guard Somoza elements and Sandinistas and in many ways, a vote for Chamorro was a vote to end the *contra* war. Not only did Chamorro have anti-Somoza bonafides, many Nicaraguans had grown tired of the Sandinista regime which had adopted at least some of the tactics of the regime it had displaced. "The Sandinistas grossly mismanaged the economy and systematically and often brutally repressed political opposition. They also engaged in personal corruption and conspicuous consumption that may well have been the most infuriating factor for the masses in whose name the revolution had been made." (67)

THE RETURN OF THE SANDINISTAS

Since losing to Violeta Chamorro in the 1990 president election, Daniel Ortega was desperate to rehabilitate his reputation and win back the presidency. After losing presidential elections in 1996 and 2001, Ortega achieved his goal and was elected president of Nicaragua in November of 2006. In a report to Congress, Maureen Taft-Morales (2007) attributes the victory of Ortega to three elements, a change in Nicaraguan electoral law which lowered the percentage of votes needed for a run-off, an effective and well-disciplined political machine and a divided opposition. (2–3) While closely aligned with Hugo Chavez and Fidel Castro, Ortega also tried to broaden his appeal by moving toward the center of the political spectrum. During the 2006 campaign Ortega often spoke of God, reconciliation and peace on the campaign trail as a strategy to expand his base beyond Sandinista voters. Also, in order to appeal to traditional Nicaraguan Catholics he married his long time female companion in a Catholic church and most importantly supported a very strict anti-abortion law that rendered abortion illegal regardless of circumstances. (Gooren 2010, 58) All of this effort helped Ortega to win the presidency and finished a transformation that had been in the making since his earlier electoral defeats. "Over the years Ortega has changed his image from Marxist revolutionary and protagonist in a proxy Cold War battle with the United States to a practicing Catholic preaching peace and reconciliation." (Taft-Morales 2007, 5)

Much of the Sandinista's electoral success is due to the ability of the party to adapt itself to changes in Nicaraguan politics and to coalescence around the leadership of Ortega. So much so that the Sandinistas "demanded unconditional loyalty to (Ortega) and expelled all those who intended to challenge him or simply disagree with him." (Puig and Wright 2010, 95) As Ortega's cult of personality, along with his personal wealth, which includes twenty-four houses and a net worth that exceeds the Somoza's at the end of the regime, (Loáisiga 2009) continues to grow, even well-known Sandinistas such as Carlos Fernando Chamorro have become opponents of the regime. "This despotic regime is bent on destroying all that is left of the Sandinista revolution's democratic legacy, standing in the way of a new dictatorship are civil society organizations, the independent media, trade unions, opposition political parties, women's organizations, civic leaders, and others—many of whom can trace their roots back to the resistance against Somoza." (Burbach 2009, 37) Part of what caused a rift between Ortega and other Sandinista leaders is Ortega's apparent transformation from a leftist revolutionary in the

1980s to a president who often governs like a center-right politician that has embraced foreign investment and free trade.

THE LEGACIES OF NICARAGUAN HISTORY

The primary legacy of Nicaraguan history and its colonization by Spain is the sharp decline in the native population and the process of *mestizaje* which radically altered the country's demographics, culture and language. "Instead of being a predominantly Indian country, [Nicaragua] is essentially mestizo in racial type and almost exclusively Spanish in language and other aspects of culture." (Walker and Wade 2011, 9). Nicaragua's experience under Spanish colonialism also planted the seeds of Nicaraguan nationalism which was affected by three main factors. The first was the defeat of Zelaya by US-backed forces which ended the possibility of a liberal revolution by the coffee elite. The second factor was the intervention of the United States which would make the main axis of conflict Nicaragua's attempts to throw of foreign dominion. Thirdly, was Sandino's vision of Indo-Hispanic nationalism in the early formation of Nicaraguan identity. (Paige 1997, 154)

It is also important to understand that the sharp decline in the native population of Nicaragua during Spanish colonialism set in motion a set of societal relationships that still affect Nicaragua today, these include very uneven development in which the Atlantic coast is far less developed than the Pacific coast. The Nicaraguan government has also long had a rocky relationship with the people of eastern Nicaragua, most notably the Miskito Indians. In addition, similarly to many other Central American countries, the area in and around the capital of Managua is the most developed part of the country, due in large part to the Somoza era which concentrated wealth in the city. In many ways, the Somoza regimes of the twentieth century were extensions of Nicaragua under colonialism in which only a small fraction of the elite received the vast majority of the country's income. Unfortunately, the current Sandinista regime under President Ortega has many of the same elements that have plagued Nicaraguan politics for its entire history, including corruption, cronyism, and the accumulation of political and economic power to a small group of elite insiders.

The most important legacy of Sandino was his focus on Nicaraguan nationalism rather than any specific ideology. Sandino's focus on nationalism was central to understanding not just Nicaragua's opposition to the US occupation, but also to the Somoza regime. In addition, the long history of outside intervention, the behavior of the Somoza regime and the struggles of the recent civil war have fostered what Mária and Arenas refer to as an "ethos of revolution" which was "ideologically shaped by Marxism and left-wing Christianity." (2009, 234) The legacy of the Somoza dynasty in particular is important to understanding modern Nicaragua as it helped to create a unique group of dissidents which included in its inspiration; Marxism, Leninism, Catholicism, nationalism, and the peoples from many different layers of Nicaraguan society. Nicaragua has also long been plagued by violent episodes, many of which culminated in the 1979 civil war. Not surprisingly, the civil war has had a long lasting legacy in Nicaragua's history and dominates much of postwar Nicaragua's politics, economics and societal relations, particularly with the reemergence of the Sandinistas in the 2006 election.

For almost all of Nicaraguan history the economy has been strikingly dependent on the outside world and "Nicaragua has been extreme case of this common phenomenon. From the days of the Spanish conquest in the sixteenth century, the Nicaraguan economy had always been externally oriented, and the people who exercised power had been the beneficiaries of this relationship." (Walker and Wade 2011, 4) As a country whose economy has been peripheral to world commerce for its entire existence, Nicaragua has found economic development very difficult based on extractive industries and agricultural exports. This fact has in turn created one of the most important legacies of Nicaraguan history, the grinding poverty that has long made life in Nicaragua very difficult.

Despite widespread poverty, as Nicaraguan history moves further and further away from the Somoza regime and the civil war, it appears more likely that the country can start anew down a different path. As Mario Arana (1995) argues, Nicaragua experienced a triple transition after the civil war:

> It was moving from war to peace and the demobilization and resettlement of previous combatants; from the restriction of civil and political rights in the face of foreign aggression and domestic discontent to a more democratic and open society that enjoyed renewed press freedom; and from a highly regulated economy and state-centered accumulation model to a market-based system undergoing neoliberal adjustment and stabilization program. (81)

These transitions are still largely an ongoing project, with the final outcome yet to be decided. The major decision points will be the extent to which the Nicaraguan government can learn from the past and apply those lessons to the future, regardless of who is in power.

THE NICARAGUAN ECONOMY

The World Bank classifies Nicaragua as a lower middle income country with a GDP per capita of $1,963 per year. Despite being one of the region's most underdeveloped countries, Nicaragua has experienced fairly rapid economic growth and rebounded from the 2008–2009 recession with a 5.4 percent growth rate in 2011. Nicaragua also has very uneven economic develop with about 80 percent of the poor living in rural areas. (World Bank 2015) This problem is especially acute given that since precolonial times most of the economic development in Nicaragua has occurred on the western side of the country with the Caribbean coast suffering the highest poverty rates in the country with very few public services. In fact,

> available socio-economic indicators show that more than 70% of the population of [Eastern Nicaragua] lives below the national poverty line and levels of unemployment reach 90%. A national poverty map produced by the Nicaraguan government in 2005 classified 12 of the 19 municipalities as extremely poor and the *costeños* lack decent access to health care, education, sanitation, drinking water, transport and telecommunications and continue to experience both institutionalized and everyday racism from Pacific Nicaraguans. (Cupples 2012, 16)

For all of Nicaraguan history it has been an agriculturally based economy centered on a small number of crops, most notably coffee. Similarly to its coffee-growing neighbors, Nicaragua developed a coffee-growing elite during the nineteenth century that long dominated politics—however in Nicaragua the coffee elite "were less likely to form great economic empires [than] those of their counterparts elsewhere in the region." (Paige 1997, 20) This meant that the coffee elite in Nicaragua, while powerful, did not have the all-encompassing power of the coffee elite in places like El Salvador. In addition, the expansion of other agricultural exports, such as cotton after World War II, further eroded the power of the coffee elite. In addition, throughout Nicaraguan history, the coffee elite were much more concerned about their own economic power and much less concerned about accruing political power and were therefore not strongly attached to the state as were the coffee elite in El Salvador. Consequently, for many coffee growers in Nicaragua there was little to like in either the Somoza regime or in the Sandinistas. In interviews with Nicaraguan coffee elites, Jeffery Paige (1997) found that the organizing principle of the Nicaraguan elite was the pursuit of liberty, namely the ability to buy and sell freely, as well as economic and political freedom. They also saw themselves at the center of both the struggle against the Somozas and later against the Sandinistas. (349) Rather than working as an enforcement arm for the economic elite as was the case with the Salvadoran military, oftentimes Nicaraguan business elites were shut out of opportunities by the Somoza family and their allies which led to many of them backing the Sandinistas during the civil war which came about because "business organizations were alienated by Somoza's monopolistic control of the economy." (Midlarsky and Roberts 1985, 178) These same Nicaraguan business elites who were alienated by the Somoza dynasty's control over the economy would later become alienated by the Sandinista's seizures of private property and similarly state-centric development model.

Not surprisingly, the civil war that started in 1979 had a devastating effect on Nicaragua's economy. "Nicaragua and its people suffered greatly as a result of the Cold War conflicts that took place in the 1980s. The country's gross domestic product (GDP) was halved, foreign debt rose more than tenfold to over US$12 billion, and a massive emigration to North America and neighbouring [*sic*] countries caused a severe decrease in the number of workers." (Pereira 2008, 164) The negative effects came not only from the level of death and destruction wrought during the war, but also from the Sandinista's mismanagement of the economy after they came to power and the difficulties inherent in paying for the war against the *contras*. When they came to power:

> The Sandinista government followed a fairly typical socialist strategy of large-scale projects intended to modernize and develop the economy. Though espousing a trickle-up form of development, which implies a basic needs strategy that would employ labor-intensive, small-scale production processes based on appropriate technology, the Sandinistas pursued a trickledown scheme. The main thrust of the government and the vast majority of its spending went to large-scale projects. (Wall 1993, 11)

This approach under the Government of National Reconstruction, which lasted from 1979 to 1985, had some level of success with economic and social policies particularly early in the regime—however, this early success would reverse itself, particularly in the face of the war against the *contras*.

> The economy went into a free fall from the mid-1980s onward, largely due to the direct and indirect cost of the Contra war and related U.S. programs of economic strangulation. But Sandinista economic policy, which became ever more erratic in the face of the hopelessness of the situation, did not help. The wild printing of unbacked currency to finance the war led to hyperinflation that passed 33,000 percent in 1988. And, though the Sandinistas themselves implemented structural reforms in that year, and the next that brought inflation down to 1,690 percent for 1989, the unemployment and social pain that those policies caused were enormous. (Walker 1997, 12)

Rather than embark on a radical socialist agenda regarding the economy, when the Sandinistas came to power they employed a mixed economy in which large portions of the economy were nationalized and consequently state-run while other enterprises were left to the private sector. Particularly galling to many of the economic elite who had been disillusioned with the Somoza regime and consequently supported the Sandinistas was that "confiscated properties were turned into state farms, peasant cooperatives, and, to a lesser extent, individual plots." (Walker 1997, 9) This "hands-on" approach, which was in some ways "bottom-up" was a radical departure from the underdevelopment of the Nicaraguan economy under the Somoza Dynasty who had been content to grow the economy only in ways that expanded their familial wealth and extended their own power.

The opening of the Nicaraguan economy after the civil war is also due to the policies of Violeta Chamorro who became the first female president in Latin America when she was elected in 1990. In the aftermath of the civil war,

> the democratic and free-market reforms begun by the Chamorro administration in the early 1990s and continued by subsequent governments yielded dramatic changes: the privatisation [*sic*] of more than 350 state enterprises, a reduction in the inflation rate from 13,500 per cent in 1991 to 9.4 per cent in 2006, and a 75 per cent reduction in foreign debt as a result of successful participation in the Highly Indebted Poor Country Initiative (HIPC) initiative. (Pereira 2008, 164)

The HIPC initiative in particular was an important step in creating economic stability in Nicaragua because "debt relief under the enhanced HIPC Initiative from all of Nicaragua's creditors will amount to approximately US$4.5 billion over time." (International Monetary Fund 2004) Despite Nicaragua's completion of the HIPC initiative, one of the biggest economic problems in Nicaragua remains the significant amount of foreign debt and the high debt servicing burden which has had a limiting effect on Nicaraguan economic growth.

While incongruent with the anti–free market rhetoric often emanating from Managua, when Daniel Ortega regained the presidency in 2006, he built upon earlier reforms to open the Nicaraguan economy and stimulate foreign direct investment as he was no doubt aware of Nicaragua's need for investment capital. The acceleration of free-market reforms since 2006 have helped Nicaragua to significantly grow its export industries, however more work is needed to make certain that Nicaraguan export industries experience consistent growth and are diversified to lower the downside from external economic shocks.

Table 2.1. Percent of growth in Nicaraguan Exports per year.

2005	2006	2007	2008	2009	2010	2011	2012	2013	2014
7.7	12.5	11.1	9	0.8	19.9	7.7	16.2	3.5	7.5

Source: World Bank.

Along with its traditional exports such as coffee and other agricultural goods, textiles have become an important export industry. This is due in large part to the ease of relocation for textile and garment facilities, government incentives to draw them to Nicaragua and a large unskilled labor force that skews younger. The Dominican Republic Central America Free Trade Agreement (DR-CAFTA) has also played a large role in economic growth. The role of DR-CAFTA in Nicaraguan economic success is ironic given how strongly it was opposed by leftist leaders throughout Latin America, particularly the Sandinistas who called it a "death certificate" for farmers and small producers and attempted to block its ratification by the previous government. Since its implementation however, Nicaragua has benefited from DR-CAFTA more than any other signatory country and asserts its role in attracting foreign investment, increasing exports and creating jobs in Nicaragua. (Rogers 2011)

Although Nicaragua has done a lot of work to change the investment environment since the end of the civil war, there are still many barriers to someone opening a business. In the World Bank's "Doing Business" rankings, Nicaragua is 125th out of 189 with the following subscores:

Table 2.2. Doing Business in Nicaragua

Activity	*DB 2016 Rank*	*DB 2015 Rank*
Starting a Business	123	119
Dealing with Construction Permits	168	164
Getting Electricity	94	90
Registering Property	147	147
Getting Credit	97	90
Protecting Minority Investors	150	149
Paying Taxes	165	163
Trading Across Borders	81	80
Enforcing Contracts	94	94
Resolving Insolvency	103	104

Source: World Bank "Doing Business" Rankings, rank out of 189.

Clearly, if Nicaragua wants to adopt a more market-oriented economy, the government needs to take steps to make it easier to open and run a business. Part of the problem is the persistence of corruption and the difficulties in securing the various licenses and permits needed to start a business. In addition, starting a business is also made difficult due to the government's harsh rhetoric and the fact that not everyone in government, particularly among anti-Ortega Sandinistas agrees with the president's attempts to attract western and especially US capital and business ventures.

THE DEVELOPMENT OF ECOTOURISM IN NICARAGUA

The most important legacy of Nicaraguan history for the pursuit of ecotourism as a development strategy is the reputation of Nicaragua based on its recent civil war. For many Americans, it is difficult to remove the image of soldiers with rifles in fatigues from their minds. Add to that a left-wing populist president who frequently engages in anti-US rhetoric and allies with US enemies, and it is easy to see why there is a general wariness among US travelers to vacation in Nicaragua. This is particularly acute given the juxtaposition of Nicaragua to Costa Rica which has long been the Central American destination of choice for US citizens. The turbulent history of Nicaragua also meant that it developed its tourism industry much later than Costa Rica, which was able to first build a domestic tourism market due to its long periods of relative peace and stability. Nicaragua developed tourism so late in its history that the first minister of tourism was not appointed until the Sandinistas came to power in 1979 under the first Ortega Administration. Given the context of the revolution and the need for new sources of income, one of their first actions was to turn some of the Somoza regime's properties into resorts. (Usher and Kerstetter 2014, 325)

Despite its turbulent history, Nicaragua has a great deal of potential for ecotourism development as it has many attractions that are of interest to tourists. "Roughly the size of Greece, at approximately 130,000 square kilometres, [*sic*] Nicaragua contains 7 per cent of the world's biodiversity and houses the second largest rainforest in the Americas—the Bosawas Rainforest Reserve." (Pereira 2008, 163) Although Nicaragua had no national parks until 1971, the country now has an extensive national park system managed by the National System of Protected Areas (SINAP) and now has 32.5 percent of Nicaraguan territory protected as of 2012. (World Bank 2015) In addition, Nicaragua has a number of cultural destinations that are of interest to tourists such as "the colonial cities of Granada and León, its majestic volcanoes, desolate beaches and peaceful fresh water lakes, as some of the last 'untouched' tourist attractions in the Americas." (Pereira 2008, 163–64) The mixture of ecological and cultural attractions provides Nicaragua an excellent starting point for both ecotourism as well as cultural tourism.

Similarly to other countries in the region, the first tourists to visit Nicaragua, particularly during the 1980s, were mostly journalists and activists—many of whom visited Nicaragua on a political tour. Since that time however and with the end of the civil war, Nicaragua "is being refashioned as the destination of another category of tourists, some adventurous and environmentally conscious and others simply eager to find an untraveled spot in the tropics." (Babb 2004, 542) Because of this trend, Nicaragua is quickly becoming a tourism hot spot. This statement from Forbes Travel Guide says a lot about American attitudes toward Nicaragua and changes to the country as well as its new identity as the "new Costa Rica":

> If the last news you heard from Nicaragua was during its years of upheaval, it's time to update your perceptions of this Central American nation, which has traded its revolutionary reputation for modern eco-tourism. With new resorts, vibrant colonial cities, powdery Pacific beaches, the world's largest freshwater volcanic island and plenty of opportunities to shop for traditional crafts, sip locally grown coffee and indulge in a chocolate massage (with Nicaraguan-produced organic cacao, of course), there are numerous reasons to consider a Nicaraguan holiday. We've got the scoop on what to do and where to go in "the new Costa Rica." (Forbes Travel Guide)

The main government agency charged with tourism development is the Instituto Nicaragüense de Turismo (INTUR) whose primary responsibilities include; developing and promoting Nicaraguan tourism around the world, encouraging investment into the tourism sector, public safety and hygiene in tourist areas and the development of human capital in the tourism sector. They are also charged with implementing and monitoring the various incentive laws for investments in tourism, the most important of which is Law #306 passed as the "Law of Incentives for the Tourism Industry of Nicaragua" in 1999 to provide a number of benefits designed to jumpstart the tourism industry. (Instituto Nicaragüense de Turismo)

One of the major goals of Law #306 was to define tourism so that investments could be targeted at specific sectors as well as create incentive systems that had as little impact as possible on the national budget. The law created development zones and authorizes the lease of state-owned properties to private investors for use as tourism sites. The main inducement for investment was a reform of Nicaraguan tax law with respect to foreign direct investment and the use of *Bonos de Inversion Turistica* (Tourist Investment Bonds) which are a form of tax increment financing that allows for the development of tourism resources without utilizing funds from the government budget. In order to benefit from this plan, the investor must operate a tourism business as defined by the law. These include hotels, restaurants, transportation, car rental, cultural activities, and infrastructure and environmental activities that relate to each of these. The primary incentive for investment in these areas are tax benefits that last for the first ten years of the project. (Instituto Nicaragüense de Turismo)

With Nicaragua's newfound focus on tourism, the country has experienced a great deal of growth in tourist arrivals over the last decade with 2014 drawing more than twice as many tourists to the country than in 2004.

Table 2.3. Tourist Arrivals to Nicaragua

Year	*Total Visitors*
2004	615,000
2005	712,000
2006	749,184
2007	799,996
2008	857,901
2009	931,904
2010	1,011,251
2011	1,060031
2012	1,179,581
2013	1,229,410
2014	1,329,663

Source: Instituto Nicaragüense de Turismo.

Due to the changes that have occurred in Nicaragua since the end of the civil war, the country is one of most popular new locations in Central America and can fill the niche once occupied by Costa Rica for travelers in search of adventure. The combination of a unique set of attributes and a low-cost tourism structure means that Nicaragua is also seen as a high-value location. In the Government of Nicaragua's National Development Plan it states that "the strategy centers on promoting and marketing tourism in order to position Nicaragua in international markets, taking advantage of our natural and cultural resources." (República de Nicaragua 1999) Nicaragua has very worked hard to develop and market itself as an ecotourism destination and given the right set of policies—ones that will consolidate gains and prepare for the future, Nicaragua can be a major ecotourism player in the region.

FOREIGN DIRECT INVESTMENT IN NICARAGUA

Throughout much of its history, Nicaragua has had a somewhat difficult time convincing foreign investors that the country is a safe destination for investment. Exacerbating this view of Nicaragua is its membership in the Bolivarian Alliance for the Peoples of Our America (ALBA) which was founded by Venezuelan president Hugo Chávez as a reaction to the signing of the Free Trade Areas of the Americas and is made up of eight countries: Nicaragua, Venezuela, Cuba, Bolivia, Dominica, Antigua and Barbuda, Ecuador, and St. Vincent and the Grenadines. Its goals are to unite the world against the prevailing world order via these three primary goals.

1. Conflict: ALBA seeks to institutionalize radical conflict (internal and external) which its member countries believe is necessary to rebuild Gran Colombia.
2. Socialism: The economic model espoused by ALBA member states is based loosely on a Trotskyite version of communism outlined by the Mexican academic Heinz Dieterich (who literally wrote the book on twenty-first century socialism). The model includes the now famous, "participatory and protagonist democracy" which involves the eventual elimination of representative democracy—and its institutional and civil-rights based approach to governance—in favor of local participation linked to a strong *caudillo* executive.
3. International Revolution: ALBA is largely a regional infrastructure designed to support the radical revolutionary processes inside member countries. The purpose of this international revolution is, as President Chávez has stated, "the creation of a new world order." According to ALBA foreign policy, the current institutional order must be brought to its knees in order to allow a new "multi-polar world" to emerge. Essential to this is the collapse of the United States as a global superpower. (Hirst 2015)

Not surprisingly, trying to attract investment from the very people that you are directly opposing is a difficult proposition. As the US Department of State's 2015 Investment Climate Statement for Nicaragua warns:

> Potential investors should be aware of the political climate, as President Ortega has previously stated that his objective in Nicaragua is to implement a socialist form of government which he defines as a mixed economy guided by Christian and socialist ideals. To achieve this balance between state and private sector participation in the economy he has used funds provided by Venezuela through the Bolivarian Alliance for the Americas (ALBA) to increase the role of the state and quasi-state actors in the economy. (3)

What is interesting about the Government of Nicaragua's membership in ALBA is that the rhetoric does not appear to constrain Nicaragua's attempts to attract foreign direct investment and even increased in 2008 after Nicaragua joined the organization the previous year.

The Ortega Administration's membership in ALBA while also attempting to attract foreign direct investment via neoliberalism, is at first glance seemingly paradoxical. However what Ortega and his allies in Nicaragua are trying to do is benefit from membership in ALBA such as petroleum concessions from Venezuela while also benefitting from outside investment. As the US State Department writes in its 2015 Investment Climate Report for Nicaragua, "To achieve this balance between state and private sector participation in the economy [President Ortega] has used funds provided by Venezuela

Table 2.4. Foreign Direct Investment in Nicaragua

Year	FDI inflows to Nicaragua in USD Millions
2004	250
2005	241.1
2006	286.8
2007	381.7
2008	627.3
2009	433.9
2010	489.9
2011	936.3
2012	767.6
2013	815.5
2014	840

Source: World Bank 2015.

through the Bolivarian Alliance for the Americas (ALBA) to increase the role of the state and quasi-state actors in the economy." (3) Undoubtedly one of the reasons the Ortega Administration has aggressively sought out foreign direct investment is that it is fully aware of the need for outside investment as Nicaraguan GDP per capita is among the lowest in the region. Outside investment is also critical since "Nicaragua's experience with alternatives to FDI is characterized by low investment levels, a currently low savings rate that has fallen into negative levels many times in the past thirty years, very high external debt, reliance on foreign aid and consistent trade deficits." (Hess 2008, 257)

Another factor that has helped to improve foreign direct investment in Nicaragua is its membership in DR-CAFTA. "Further improving the climate for outside investment was a group of reforms passed by the Nicaraguan legislature as a complement to the treaty that served to take full advantage of the international market opening." (Feinberg 2008, 163) Known as the complimentary agenda, it

> addressed a wide range of national competitiveness measures, including measures to make markets more efficient, render the government more effective, and spread the benefits more widely. Market-perfecting measures included a competition law intended to protect smaller firms, land titling to ensure property rights for small landowners, and stronger institutions to promote international standards in agricultural certification. State modernization goals included an online land registry, information systems for smaller firms, budge-

> tary resources for the Ministry of Labor, customs facilitation, and alternative dispute resolution mechanisms. To foster wider participation in CAFTA's marketing opportunities, the Nicaraguan Congress proposed new rural road systems and technology transfer to small firms. (163)

When Ortega reassumed the presidency in the 2006 presidential elections, there were some questions as to whether DR-CAFTA and other pro-business legislation would survive. This question was put to rest when President Ortega reaffirmed his support for DR-CAFTA and its complimentary agenda. (163) The primary government agency in charge of managing many of these incentives and attracting investment to Nicaragua is ProNicaragua which "was founded in 2002 in an alliance between the Government of Nicaragua, the United Nations Development Programme (UNDP), the Multilateral Investment Guarantee Agency of the World Bank (MIGA), and Harvard Business School, through its Service Leadership Fellows Program." (Pereira 2008, 167) While ProNicaragua seeks to attract foreign direct investment similarly to other investment promotion agencies around the world, it does so with an eye to job creation rather than economic growth for its own sake. This is due in large part to the comparative advantage of Nicaragua's large, young and inexpensive labor force. As such, ProNicaragua has taken the lead in bringing garment industry jobs, which some states such as Costa Rica have rejected, to Nicaragua which tend to be highly mobile and seek out inexpensive low-skilled labor.

ProNicaragua offers a number of incentives to attract investors with the main body of law centered on tax incentives in export-oriented operations including agriculture. In addition, there are a number of tax benefits for export industries for the purchase of equipment and partially finished goods. The main system of tax and development incentives offered by ProNicaragua is via the Industrial Free Zones for Export (Decree 46–91) Under this arrangement the Government of Nicaragua offers tax incentives for businesses that want to establish an export-oriented operation in the textiles and clothing industries, manufacturing, agriculture and call centers. The incentives offered under this law include a 100 percent exemption from payment of income tax for the first ten years and 60 percent thereafter. In addition, there are a number of exemptions for expenses related to establishing and running a business in the Industrial Free Zone. (ProNicaragua 2015)

ProNicaragua also manages the Incentives for the Tourism Industry Law which seeks to boost tourism in Nicaragua by offering a variety of tax incentives and coves incentives and benefits for investment in accommodation, food and beverage, tour operators, tourist transportation and airlines. These benefits include exemption from 80 to 100 percent of yearly income tax for ten years, a 100 percent exemption from property value added tax applicable to design services, engineering and construction and import tax and duty on the purchase of materials and fixtures of the building each for up to ten years. In addition, if at the end of first ten-year period at least 35 percent of the original investment amount is reinvested it is possible to receive can receive each of the benefits and exemptions for a further ten years. (ProNicaragua 2015) These incentives for outside investment coupled Nicaragua's membership in DR-CAFTA mean that the country's dedication to embracing globalization and embarking on neoliberal reforms is far different than it appears at first glance. It will be interesting to see if these policies would survive if a member of the Sandinista Party besides Daniel Ortega was elected president.

FACTORS THAT ENCOURAGE ECOTOURISM DEVELOPMENT AND FOREIGN DIRECT INVESTMENT

Given Nicaragua's long history of upheaval and image in the minds of many Americans, the growth of both tourist arrivals and foreign direct investment is nothing short of miraculous. They have been able to accomplish this by creating an atmosphere that is welcoming to tourists and investors alike as they have opened Nicaragua to the world. While the growth of tourism and outside investment has been substantial, there are still many daunting tasks that remain if Nicaragua is to achieve its full potential. Given the high poverty rate in Nicaragua and its recent economic growth, it is critical for the government of Nicaragua to make the most out of the country's progress over the last two decades. Not only is this a unique opportunity for Nicaragua, but tourism is also uniquely positioned to benefit. For instance, Croes and Vanegas (2008) found that there is a "long-run stable relationship among tourism development, economic expansion, and poverty reduction exists for Nicaragua [and] foreign exchange earnings from international tourism positively affects Nicaraguan economic expansion and reduce its poverty." (102) Despite the bright outlook for Nicaragua, there is still a lot of work to do. One important issue is the development of democracy over the long-term and a continuing dedication to the rule of law. While President Ortega and the Sandinistas look as though they are dedicated to democracy and Ortega in particular has opened Nicaragua to the outside world via free-market reforms, for many tourists and investors, there are still lingering doubts.

These doubts are exacerbated by Nicaragua's continued membership in ALBA, whose anti-American and anti-globalization rhetoric stand at odds with the reality of large-scale US investment and increasing tourism to Nicaragua. In fact, on ProNicaragua's website tries to appeal to US investors by stating that "for historical reasons, there is a cultural affinity with the United States" (ProNicaragua 2015) In addition, since Ortega has routinely changed the rules of the game to put himself into and then stay in power, it sends a counterproductive message regarding the rule of law. Another issue that needs to be resolved is the so-called *No Pago* movement in Nicaragua which caused a crisis among microlenders in the aftermath of the 2008–2009 global financial crisis. These issues reflect poorly on the rule of law in Nicaragua and President Ortega would be well served to either cease with the rhetoric or pull Nicaragua out of ALBA completely.

There are also structural issues that affect the rule of law, including a number of issues related to the enforcement of contracts. "While the Nicaraguan government seeks to increase economic growth in part by increasing foreign investment, the country's weak judicial system, land titling issues, and corruption create serious challenges for businesses operating in Nicaragua." (US Department of State 2015, 3) There are also concerns that Nicaragua's attempt to build a transoceanic canal will negatively affect property rights. This general fear was exacerbated by the granting of a concession to build the canal to a Chinese-based company, who will be allowed to compensate those that lose property in a way that has investors worried that if their property is seized they will not be adequately compensated.

> In 2013 the Nicaraguan government granted the Hong Kong Nicaragua Development Group (HKND) a 100-year concession to build the proposed canal with no competition and no opportunity for public comment. The Nicaraguan law that grants the canal concession states that property owners will be paid at "cadastral value," which U.S. investors fear will be below fair market value and in violation of the Nicaraguan government's obligations under the Free Trade Agreement between the United States, Central America, and the Dominican Republic (CAFTA-DR). (3)

One significant positive event was Nicaragua's ratification of DR-CAFTA, which should be an important step toward improving the country's investment climate. In addition, "Nicaragua has implemented measures that provide improved protection of personal and intellectual property and grant equal treatment for local and foreign investors, and allow the free repatriation of profits and capital." (Pereira 2008, 164) These actions are especially important given Nicaragua's association with the rhetoric of ALBA and the Sandinista's history of the expropriation of private property during the civil war when approximately 28,000 properties were seized. (US Department of State 2015, 6)

DR-CAFTA and other measures to strengthen the rule of law have also played a major role in liberalizing the Nicaraguan economy, which in turn has led directly to a large increase in investment. This openness to investment came to fruition based on a concerted effort by the government of Nicaragua to engage in the globalized economy because of their desperate need for capital investment. Given Nicaragua's history and some of its allies, DR-CAFTA did a lot to both quell investor fear and open the Nicaraguan economy to the outside world.

> The CAFTA-DR Investment Chapter establishes a secure, predictable legal framework for U.S. investors in Central America and the Dominican Republic. The agreement provides six basic protections: (1) nondiscriminatory treatment relative to domestic investors and investors from third countries; (2) limits on performance requirements; (3) the free transfer of funds related to an investment; (4) protection from expropriation other than in conformity with customary international law; (5) a minimum standard of treatment in conformity with customary international law; and (6) the ability to hire key managerial personnel without regard to nationality. (4)

Tourists will be more likely to visit because, despite its turbulent history, "Nicaragua today is paradoxically one of the safest countries in Latin America." (Pereira 2008, 163) In fact, Nicaragua compares favorably to Costa Rica, a country with the reputation for being a stable and safe place to visit and often the first place US citizens visit in the region. An important factor in Nicaragua's lower crime rate is that the drug wars which have plagued Mexico and many parts of Central America have never really reached into Nicaragua. This is due in large part to massive reforms to the police apparatus during the 1990s in the aftermath of the civil war. One of the most important changes is that the government has been able to maintain its monopoly on violence as "a combination of factors encapsulated in its complex transition [to democracy] allowed Nicaragua to produce security institutions that although far from perfect, are more effective in controlling their own violent entrepreneurs." (Cruz 2011, 25)

Despite its low overall crime rate, crime in Nicaragua is still prevalent in and around Managua and is also higher in the tourist cities of Granada and Masayo, though still lower than comparable cities in the region. "Although Nicaragua has critical issues regarding public security, any comparison with Guatemala, El Salvador, and Honduras exhibits a clear difference in terms of the prevalence of crime. Indeed, the levels of violence in Nicaragua are closer to those of Costa Rica, a longstanding democracy, than to those of other transitional countries." (2) The comparison to Costa Rica is interesting and speaks to the cultural changes that have occurred in Nicaragua with respect to the use of violence as the two lowest crime countries in Central America are Costa Rica (the wealthiest) and Nicaragua (the poorest). Similarly to Costa Rica, Nicaragua "created a tourism police unit that is deployed to areas frequented by tourists and maintains a 24 hour hotline for emergencies." (United States Department of State Bureau of Diplomatic Security Nicaragua Report 2015) This should go a long way to making visiting tourists feel safer.

Interestingly, while many governments try to draw foreign direct investment based on an educated workforce, Nicaragua tries to do so based more on its ability to deliver a low-skill (and low-cost) workforce. For instance, the US State Department in Investment Climate Statement for Nicaragua states that "Nicaragua focuses the majority of its efforts on attracting companies that require low skilled labor because unskilled labor is widely available and low cost. In addition, the Nicaraguan population is very young with 76 percent of the population under 39 years old." (2015, 3) While this formula might be effective for outside investment in areas like the garment industry, in order to build the type of human capital necessary for an ecotourism industry, it is necessary for the government of Nicaragua to improve its education system. For this, Nicaragua could look to Costa Rica as a model for the training of wildlife guides to ensure sustainable ecotourism has an educational element.

One of the most important areas in need of improvement is English language instruction. Due to Nicaragua's proximity to the United States, English language skills among its hospitality workers are especially vital to the increasing the number of visitors from the United States. One of the main emphases on ProNicaragua's website is the growing number of Nicaraguans studying English. It states:

> According to a study carried out by ProNicaragua about the Spanish and English speaking population, showed that the interest of Nicaraguan[s] in speaking English as a second language is growing fast. The results of the study showed that in 2013, there were almost 23,000 students learning English in public and private language centers; furthermore, almost 9,300 students finished the study program. (ProNicaragua 2015)

While over 32,000 students studying English may sound like a large number, Nicaragua has a population of around six million people. In addition to English language skills, there is also a lot of room for improvement in Spanish literacy as Nicaragua's literacy rate is 82.8 percent among those fifteen years and older with virtually equal rates between men and women (CIA World Factbook). These problems stem from a Nicaraguan educational system that has long suffered problems of funding, attendance and poor student performance and has been a near constant target of reform by various IGOs, NGOs and the Nicaraguan government.

Despite the Sandinista's use of Nicaraguan schools as political fodder, the Ortega Administration has funded education at the lowest percentage of GDP in Central America—spending an average of 3.5 percent of GDP per year on average compared to 6 percent in Honduras and 8 percent in Costa Rica. (Hutt) Attendance has also been problematic among Nicaraguan students and enforcement is lax. In addition, many families have a difficult time paying the various fees required for their children to attend school and too often students do not attend or drop out altogether so they can go to work to provide supplemental income to their families. The most startling shortfall however is in student performance—of 2,400 student who took admissions exams at National Engineering University, only 136 passed a basic mathematic test and only 2.3 percent of applicants passed the admissions exam for National Autonomous University of Nicaragua. (Hutt) Given these issues, education is a major barrier to economic development in Nicaragua and is particularly acute in the skillset needed for effective sustainable ecotourism development.

Like many of its neighbors, Nicaragua's infrastructure is badly in need of upgrade and repairs. The World Economic Forum ranks Nicaragua 116 out of 142 for its infrastructure. (World Economic Forum) The most controversial part of Nicaragua's infrastructure plan is the construction of an isthmian canal to compete with the Panama Canal. From the beginning this project has caused a great deal of apprehension given its cost and ability to compete with the Panama Canal. In addition, several groups both inside and outside of Nicaragua have stepped forward to oppose the construction of a canal.

> A loose coalition of more than 30 concerned groups filed legal complaints with the government of Nicaragua in the second half of last year. These included three communities—the Miskitu and Ulwa indigenous peoples and the Rama-Kriol territorial government in the South Atlantic Autonomous Region—arguing that the canal concession violates their land rights and legal autonomy. These legal petitions were overridden by the National Assembly in December. (Meyer and Huete-Pérez 2014, 289)

The new Nicaraguan canal is planned to exceed the size of the Panama Canal at a cost of US$40 billion. Though cost overruns can be expected to be 50 to 100 percent of the estimate (Condit 2015, 1), the government of Nicaragua hopes the canal will help to spur the economy via revenue and jobs created, both in its construction as well as its operation. Part of this optimism comes from the success of Panama in running their canal after it was repatriated in 1999. A second major concern inherent in Nicaragua's plan to build a new canal is the environmental implications. This issue is particularly stark given both Nicaragua's attempts to build sustainable ecotourism and the fact that "the current state of the environment in Nicaragua is so threatened that remaining forests are likely to disappear in a matter of decades." (6)

Given the necessity of the natural environment to sustainable ecotourism, it is extremely important for the government of Nicaragua to put more stringent environmental regulations in place that can help to preserve what is left of the natural environment. In addition, while it is no doubt tempting to build a project such as the canal due to the possibility of huge amounts of outside investment, Nicaraguan politicians would be better off pursuing other avenues of investment, particularly those that will preserve the environmental and allow Nicaraguan to develop a viable and profitable sustainable ecotourism industry.

While it seems somewhat unlikely that a canal through Nicaragua could be built, its construction, or even an attempt at its construction, could have devastating effects on ecotourism. The Association for Tropical Biology and Conservation found that the canal will affect approximately 4,000 square kilometers of forest, coast, and wetlands—many of which are currently under some form of environmental protection. (Fonseca, 2015) While the ultimate construction of the canal could push Nicaragua away from the type of environmental conservation necessary for a viable ecotourism industry, the real danger is that a partially built canal will destroy the possibility of ecotourism without creating any economic benefit.

COMPARATIVE ADVANTAGES AND FUTURE PROSPECTS

In an article discussing how to market the various countries of Central America to US travelers, *Travel Agent* magazine states that "if you are going [to Nicaragua], you are more of a pioneer-type of traveler. That's not your first jump into Latin America. You have some stamps on your passport. It's probably for an adventurous couple and we don't get a lot of people bringing young kids there. You're a bit more of an explorer." (Pike 2015, 11) Because of this, Nicaragua has a chance to fill the ecotourism niche which was once the (nearly) exclusive domain of Costa Rica. Similarly to Costa Rica twenty years ago, the primary comparative advantage for sustainable ecotourism in Nicaragua is price and value and the idea of adventure. In order to capitalize on this comparative advantage it is necessary for Nicaragua to implement changes that will improve the safety, infrastructure, and overall tourist experience for visitors. In addition, it is vital that the government of Nicaragua enact policies that can preserve the natural environment so it can be used for sustainable ecotourism.

Another important issue for Nicaragua, particularly under the Sandinistas, is how to reconcile their membership in ALBA with a free-market oriented neoliberal economy. The apparent drift in Ortega's politics since the 1980s combines leftist, anticapitalist, and anti-American rhetoric with an economy that is open with a large number of investments from the United States. However, while it might be possible for the Sandinistas under Ortega to "have it both ways" and accrue benefits from countries in ALBA—for instance the petroleum concessions they receive from Venezuela—balancing anti-American, antiglobalization, and antineoliberalism rhetoric with lots of American investment in a globalized and neoliberalism-oriented Nicaraguan economy could prove a very difficult feat. Not only could the incongruence in words and actions infuriate the Nicaraguan people, the ALBA-inspired political rhetoric could certainly scare of potential foreign investors. Given the history and rhetoric of Sandino as well as the Sandinistas in modern Nicaragua, it is truly amazing that the country in many ways exemplifies the benefits of engaging in neoliberal policy and benefitting from a globalized economy. This apparent transformation of Daniel Ortega, and to a lesser extent the Sandinistas generally, from Socialist revolutionaries to free market (almost), center-right politicians is one of the most remarkable political transformations in post–Cold War Latin American politics.

Chapter Three

Belize: Top Competitor to Costa Rica

Over the last couple of decades Belize has emerged as one of the world's hottest locations for ecotourism and adventure travel. Over that time, Belize has also worked hard to develop community-based development programs that strongly encourages average Belizeans to have a stake in the ecotourism industry. An important part of Belize's burgeoning success is due to its interesting combination of natural and cultural attractions that speak to the country's unique history. One of the most important factors in Belize's ascendency to ecotourism hot spot is the fact that Belize is an English-speaking country which helps to make it an amenable location for tourists from the United States and Canada. Despite Belize's many positive attributes, there is still a lot for the country to work on to become a modern efficient economy that is able to encourage long-term economic growth. Particularly troubling is the endemic corruption felt across virtually every aspect of Belizean politics. In a report written for the Central Bank of Belize Ydahlia Metzgen (2012) sums up the Belizean economy by describing it as "a small, highly open, natural resource and services-based, export economy, currently dependent on petroleum, agriculture and tourism services and overburdened with external debt. The state sector in Belize represents about one-third of the economy while the private sector accounts for two-thirds." (5) This unique set of attributes and liabilities situates Belize as a very interesting case study.

PRECOLONIAL BELIZE

The Mayans settled and lived in what would become Belize starting approximately 2000 BC and established one of the great civilizations of history. "During the roughly six-century period of their florescence, from about 250–900 AC, the Maya created a civilization in a tropical, low-land setting, a civilization that was characterized by elaborate art and architectural styles, complex calendrical and hieroglyphics systems, long-distance trade networks for exotic goods, and spectacular ceremonial centers." (Healy, Lambert, Arnason, and Hebda 397, 1983) Covering an area from western Honduras through Guatemala to the Yucatán Peninsula of southern Mexico, Belize was one of the central locations of Mayan culture and contained several important Mayan city-states such as Caracol and Altun Ha. The Maya in Belize, like elsewhere, were a loosely knit group of city-states that shared many common characteristics, but were not a united political entity.

For reasons that scholars do not yet fully understand, the Maya population throughout Central America went into a decline around 1000 AD from which they would not recover. Throughout the Mayan world after 1000 AD "public building activity ceased, the administrative centers lost power, and the population declined as social and economic systems lost their coherence." (Bolland 1986, 10) While the greatness of Maya culture waned, "many Maya were still present in Belize when the Europeans came in the sixteenth and seventeenth centuries." (11) Part of the reason the Spaniards were never particularly interested in bringing Belize fully into the colonial system was that the area was relatively sparsely populated and the Maya that lived there did so in very rugged territory that made conquest very difficult. Estimates of the number of Mayan peoples in Belize when the Spaniards arrived ranges from 50,000 to 400,000. (Thomson 2004, 8)

SPAIN AND GREAT BRITAIN

Similarly to the majority of Central and South America, the Spaniards were the first to make landfall in what would become Belize when Christopher Columbus reached the southeast corner of the Bay of Honduras on his fourth trip to the New World in 1502. (Menon 1979, 344) With much better opportunities for colonization in other parts of Latin America and the paucity of easily exploitable resources in Belize, the Spaniards were not particularly interested in settling or even governing the region, though this did not stop Spain from claiming possession over Belize, which was, in their estimation, given to them by Pope Alexander I in 1493 when Columbus set off on his first journey. (344)

Despite only marginal interest in the region, throughout much of the sixteenth and seventeenth centuries Spain would periodically raid Belize from the Yucatán peninsula of Mexico in order to subdue it, but was never able to bring the area under its full control due to strong opposition from the Maya and would usually quickly give up. These half-hearted raids by the Spaniards and their inability to bring Belize fully under its control were one of the early factors that made Belize a refuge for people fleeing Spanish colonialism. (Bolland 1986, 12) A second reason the area was able to serve as a refuge from the Spaniards was the rugged nature of the terrain which often truncated the Spaniards efforts at subjugating the local Maya. In addition to these military raids, Spain would also occasionally send missionaries to Belize to convert the population to Roman Catholicism and sometimes built churches in an attempt to leave a permanent presence. For the most part, these efforts were unsuccessful—so much so that modern Belize has one of the lowest percentages of Roman Catholics among former colonies of Spain.

This initial lack of interest would actually come back to haunt Spain because in addition to serving as a safe haven for Mayan peoples escaping the Spaniards, it also "formed a perfect base for British buccaneers raiding Spanish shipping." (Petch 1986, 1002) Although the buccaneer's raids against Spain certainly assisted Britain's geopolitical goals of that era, the British settlement of Belize by "Baymen" as the settlers were called, was not expressly endorsed or aided by the British government and Belize did not have a crown representative until formally granted colony status by the British in 1862. (Curry 1956, 32) The Baymen would also put in place an economic system in which they controlled the vast majority of land and slaves in the area which was somewhat distinct from slavery in other parts of the New World. "In Belize a handful of white settlers, or 'Baymen,' faced repeated internal challenges to their control of timber resources and the African slave labor they employed to exploit them. Founded as an enclave for the shipment of logwood, and later mahogany, to European markets, Belize was a slave society distinct from the plantation economies of the British West Indies." (Moberg 1992, 2)

Throughout its time as a colony, slavery played an important role in the development of Belize, particularly in the growth of British power there. As Everitt (1986) argues, "[Slavery] undoubtedly contributed to the fact that by the end of the first quarter of the eighteenth century, the British were dominant throughout the logwood trade." (79) The settlement of the British in Central America not only threatened the economic prospects of Spain, but the buccaneers themselves engaged in widespread looting against Spanish settlements along with their logging endeavors. The British settlement of Belize helped to push Spain into a series of treaties, the most important of which was the Godolphin Treaty of 1670 which "provided for the maintenance of peace between the kings of Britain and Spain and prohibited the subjects of either king from sailing and trading in any place whatsoever in the West Indies possessed by the other." (Menon 1979, 346) Not surprisingly, the Godolphin Treaty did little to quell the conflict between Spain and Britain and the fighting over Belize continued for most of the next hundred years until the Treaty of Versailles in 1783 and the influx of British settlers starting in 1780s.

As Spain's power waned throughout their colonies there was little they could do to quell British incursions in Central America and the Caribbean. The last attempt of Spain to attack British settlements in Belize was in 1798 at the Battle of St. George's Caye which ended in abject failure for the Spaniards and marked an end to their interests there. In addition, the wars of independence in Latin America which ejected Spain from most of the region by 1816 allowed Britain (among others) to encroach upon areas formally controlled by the Spaniards. The waning power of Spain and its eventual eviction from Latin America coupled with the weakness of the Central American Federation in the years after independence allowed the borders of British Honduras to expand to its current size.

BRITISH HONDURAS

British settlement of Belize reached its critical mass with the formation of the British Honduras Company in 1859. This did not, however, bring an end to the disputed nature of the British presence in Central America nor its various border disputes, most importantly with Guatemala, who, despite signing a treaty with Great Britain to determine the precise borders of British Honduras, thought Belize's territory belonged to them. The root of the problem was that Guatemala considers Belize to be the illegitimate infant of the British Caribbean empire and that it rightfully should be a part of Guatemala. (Curry 1956, 31) The legal basis for this claim, according to Guatemala, is that Spain never officially relinquished the idea that Belize was its territory when they left, and as such the Guatemalan government has always held that the territorial claim over Belize passed to newly independent Guatemala. Not even when the British made Belize (then known as British Honduras) a formal colony in 1862, did the disputes over the rightful ruler of Belize end. The organization of the British Honduras Company also began a change in the economic landscape of Belize in which the original settlers would slowly lose their grip on power. "The British Honduras Company, later renamed the Belize Estate and Produce Company, emerged as the predominant landowner. It had about half of all privately-held land in the colony. And the company became the dominant force in British Honduras' political and economic life for more than a century." (Mwakikagile 2014, 39)

Despite its longtime status as a "backwater" of the European powers that colonized it, Belize did provide certain geopolitical advantages for those that ruled it. The British for their part, were mostly interested in keeping Belize not because of the economic benefit, but rather because it represented their only foothold in Central America. "Belize was an economic borderland of the main European powers in the New World. Colonial British Honduras never garnered the attention bestowed on the other British colonies in North

America, the Caribbean, Africa and India. Because it was essentially a depopulated area, there was hardly any economic advantage to the British staying there. Nevertheless it was their foothold in Central America, and they stayed," (Sutherland, 1998, 17) This desire to keep a foothold in Latin America and the Caribbean accelerated as the United States started to flex its foreign policy muscles in the region.

The formal organization of British Honduras as a Crown Colony under a new constitution in 1871 once and for all transferred power from the descendants of those who had settled or migrated there to British colonial authorities in Jamaica and London.

> Under the new constitution, Belize was governed by the governor-in-council with a council consisting of five official and four unofficial members, all nominated. This constitutional change confirmed and completed a change in the locus and form of power in the colony's political economy that had been evolving during the preceding half century. (Bolland 1986, 24)

While this arrangement had its drawbacks for those living in British Honduras, the loss of some level of control was somewhat mitigated by the protections inherent in becoming a full-fledged British colony. In addition, the change to Crown Colony status in 1871 also changed the political organization of the colony as the Legislative Assembly, which had been established only seventeen years before was abolished as the British Crown sought to exercise a more direct control over the colony by switching to a wholly appointed rather than elected Legislative Council. (22–3)

The time between Belize becoming a Crown Colony in 1871 and the onset of the Great Depression was dominated by the consolidation of land and capital into the hands of a small European elite as the fortunes of the timber industry waxed and waned. The continued focus on logging, particularly the lucrative mahogany trade, also served to limit the number of crops cultivated in Belize. This meant that similar to its neighbors throughout the region, Belize was especially prone to the cyclical nature of the dependence on a small number of agricultural exports. This problem, inherent in this dependence, meant that the Great Depression hit Belize especially hard and unemployment grew rapidly. "The *Colonial Report for 1931* stated that 'the contracts for the purchase of mahogany and chicle, which form the mainstay of the Colony, practically ceased altogether, thereby throwing a large number of the woodcutters and chicle-gatherers out of work.'" (32) The Great Depression and the general economic stagnation of Belize and the conflict over the structure of the colonial regime and which parts should or should not be elected by the people rather than appointed were important parts in what would become the Belizean independence movement.

BELIZEAN SELF-GOVERNMENT AND INDEPENDENCE

Between the mid-1930s and 1964 there were several political changes that put Belize on the road to independence. The major change to the government of Belize was the granting of self-government by the British in 1964.

> Full internal self-government was provided by a constitution that created a bicameral legislature, the National Assembly, consisting of House of Representatives of eighteen elected members and a Senate of eight nominated members . . . between 1964 and 1981, the British government retained authority through the governor over foreign affairs, defense, internal security, and the terms and conditions of appointment of the civil service. (107)

In 1973 British Honduras officially changed its name to Belize and in 1981 become a fully independent state recognized by the United Nations.

Interestingly, the biggest problems faced by Belize for its independence did not come from the British who had worked hard to find a way to facilitate Belizean independence, but from the Guatemalans who had never given up the idea that Belize should be a part of Guatemala, in fact, the Guatemalan constitution of 1945 states that "Belice" is the twenty-third department of Guatemala. (131) When Belize was a British colony, British government officials would periodically engage in fruitless talks with the Guatemalan government to agree on a demarcation of the border that would solve the dispute

In addition to the territorial dispute with Guatemala, which delayed Belizean independence, Belize also has a number of other problems as a small, isolated, and resource-poor Central American state that bore little resemblance to its neighbors, one of which did not think it should exist at all. In an article written for *World Affairs* in 1975, Paula Herman points out the various difficulties in Belizean independence:

> Guatemala has persisted in her claim and has publicized her intention to seize the territory as soon as British forces withdraw. The magnitude of the Guatemalan challenge can be appreciated when the situation is examined. Guatemala has a population 40 times larger than British Honduras, a Gross Domestic Product 36 times larger, and an army and air force which are considered to be the best in Central America. British Honduras has neither an army nor an air force, nor has she currently the resources with which to raise either. In light of this situation, British Honduras has refused to accept external self-government without a defense guarantee. Britain has been adamant in her refusal to make such a long-term commitment. Canada, Mexico, and the United States, to whom British Honduras has also looked for defense guarantees, have also refused to make commitments. (61)

Given these problems, Herman then sums up Belize's viability as an independent state:

> After an exploration of the physical setting, the human setting, and the political setting of British Honduras, it must be concluded that she is not a potentially viable state. She possesses no significant mineral resources, no significant industrial development, an underdeveloped agricultural sector, a declining forestry industry, and a stronger neighbor who claims her entire territory. Her population is poorly educated and divided into several distinct and frequently antagonistic groups. Her political system is characterized by a nascent split along ethnic lines which prevents agreement on basic questions of national identity. There is little basis for a prediction of viability should she achieve full independence. (67)

Despite these dire predictions, when Belize finally became independent it was due to international pressure, the involvement of the United Nations and the agreement with the British to leave a defense force in place to dissuade the Guatemalans from invading. With these factors in place, members of the United Nations voted 139 in favor, none opposed, with seven abstentions, of a resolution to secure independence for Belize, with Guatemala refusing to vote. (Bolland 1986, 134) Guatemala did finally recognize Belizean independence in 1992, which allowed the British forces protecting them to withdraw in 1994.

POST-INDEPENDENCE BELIZE

The Belizean constitution, written in 1981 is very similar to the institutional structure under British colonialism and self-rule and continued the tradition of a parliamentary system with a bicameral legislature and an independent judiciary. At the time of its independence, Belize had long been dominated politically by George Cadle Price who had been head of government under the British from 1961 to 1981. He was able to build a political movement around the idea of Belizean nationalism and the need for democracy and autonomy for Belizean officials who had long been subservient to a laidback British colonial authority in London. Price was also the founder of one of the two major political parties in Belize, the People's United Party (PUP). Early leaders of the PUP aligned themselves with organized labor and as such the PUP was founded as a center-left Christian Democratic party in 1950. As the luminary figure of the early national period in Belizean politics, "the event that precipitated the formation of PUP and George Price's career was the devaluation of the British Honduran Dollar on 31 December 1949 [which] provided an opportunity for various labor and nationalist forces to rally around a clear issue." (114)

For much of Belize's history under self-rule and then for the first post-independence election, the PUP were elected to a majority of political offices with Price serving as Belize's first prime minister after independence, serving until 1984 and again in 1989. Despite the PUP's electoral success as Belize's dominant party of the early national period, starting in the 1970s, the PUP's popularity started to erode when three smaller parties joined forces to create the United Democratic Party (UDP) as a center-right alternative to the PUP. (122) The formation of the UDP also led to the victory of Manuel Esquivel in the 1984 Belizean elections. The political landscape of Belize since independence has seen each party alternate control over the prime minister's office, except for consecutive victories in 2008 and 2012 for the UDP.

THE LEGACIES OF BELIZEAN HISTORY

Throughout the history of Belize it has long been underpopulated, was loosely governed by colonial powers, and was often ignored altogether. British author Aldous Huxley once said, "If the world had any ends British Honduras would be one of them. It is not on the way from anywhere to anywhere else" (1950, 35) Due to its location and lax colonial administration, Belize was able to develop a unique ethnic mixture. The unique demographics of Belize are due to several historical factors—including its place as a safe haven by those fleeing violence and oppression in the region in the colonial period, the various groups that migrated to the country either voluntarily or involuntarily including colonists from Spain and Great Britain, African slaves and in later years Mennonites and those fleeing the region's civil wars in the 1980s.

While the majority ethnic groups in Belize are mestizo and those of Spanish descent, there are also a sizable number of Mayan peoples as well as the Garifuna. (CIA World Factbook) The Mayan peoples originate from both inside as well as outside Belize and represent an important minority group in the country. One of the most unique ethnic groups are the Garifuna who are a mix of Arawak and Carib Indians and people of African descent. The exact origin of the Garifuna is still considered a contested issue even among the Garifuna themselves—although there is a general agreement that their origins can be traced to a shipwreck in in 1635 in which a number of African slaves escaped to St. Vincent and intermarried with the indigenous people there. For much of the colonial period, the St. Vincent area of Belize served as a safe haven for escaped slaves from other parts of Spanish America. (Sutherland 1998, 22–23) Given their historical roots, the modern Garifuna "combine African phenotypic features with Amerindian cultural and linguistic characteristics." (Moberg 1992, 3)

The introduction of the Garifuna and the various diasporas of the Maya from other parts of Central America played a very important part in the development of Belizean society as their labor was greatly valued in a colony that was not particularly labor-rich. The fact that Belize did not have a large labor force meant that the region did not develop the same sort of forced labor systems, known as *encomiendo* or *repartimiento* that were implemented by the Spaniards in the Yucatán as well as in other parts of Central America, most notably in Guatemala. Further exacerbating the need to more pragmatically manage these groups rather than to oppress them through the use of forced labor arrangements was that not only was their labor needed, but the Garifuna in particular had a reputation for aggression and were somewhat feared by colonial authorities. As Moberg (1992) argues, "Indigenous peoples such as the Garifuna and Maya that were both needed for their labor and also feared as unwilling subjects resulted in pragmatic political approaches to their administration." (4) These more pragmatic approaches to colonization is an important legacy of colonialism in Belize and in many ways define modern societal relations.

One important effect of Belize's colonial experience and its unique ethnic makeup is that modern Belize is still searching for a coherent single Belizean identity. The lack of a pervasive forced labor system means that ethnic relations do not have many of the features of ethnic and class relations in places like Guatemala, which has experienced long bouts of racial and ethnic violence including a thirty-six-year civil war. Not only does Belize not have a similar history of racialized politics, in Belize the push for "nationhood was primarily a matter of political rhetoric, government commissions, and debate among the educated elite." (Wilk 1999, 244)

The fact that Belize spent a long period of its history as an English-speaking British colony coupled with the unique ethnic makeup also gives Belize an air of illegitimacy to some in Central America and the mix of ethnic groups and colonizing countries has made creating a Belizean identity difficult. Country Watch (2015) concludes that Belize suffers from both an external identity crisis as an English outlier in a region of former Spanish colonies and international diversity that makes creating a Belizean identity difficult.

> The history of Belize involves the outward struggle to establish and maintain an English-speaking nation in an area dominated by Latino peoples and culture, and the inward interaction between groups of different races and cultural backgrounds. Understanding contemporary social relations and the politics of Belize depends on understanding these diverse groups and their interpretations of past events. Despite the gradual emergence of a national identity, the differences among ethnic groups and their divergent outlooks on the present and the past play an important role in Belize today. (7)

While Belize certainly suffers from many of the same problems as its neighbors—such as income and land inequality—for the most part these problems are not as acute as in other places in Latin America. Belize bears some resemblance to Costa Rica as each country had a relatively mild colonial experience compared to other countries in Central America. The similarity between Belize and Costa Rica is borne of the evolution of over three hundred years of forced labor under Spanish colonialism in places like Guatemala and Peru and its absence in Belize and Costa Rica. Furthermore, in much of Belize and Costa Rica it was necessary to engage in a wage labor system because of the acute labor shortages in each place. The differences in ethnic relations in Belize and Costa Rica versus many of its neighbors is a result of the difference between forced labor and wage labor over the course of Spanish colonialism. All of this means that "Belize lacks the violent class and racial conflict that has figured so prominently in the social life of its Central American neighbors." (Metzgen 2012, 29)

Economically Belize has spent its entire history on the periphery of the world's economy and has been beholden to a range of economic forces under which they had no control. For most of Belize's experience under British colonialism, the Belizean economy was one in which "production followed the dictates of trade, as the British markets, merchants, and investors determined what Belizeans would produce and how much they would get for it." (Bolland 1986, 69–70) This subservience to outside economies continued when Belize became independent and since that time the country relied on a small number of exports which for the most part have been determined by the needs of the international market. In addition, Belize represents an even more extreme example of something that is common throughout the region: states that export raw materials while importing almost all of their finished goods. One key difference between Belize and many of its neighbors is that for a good deal of its history Belize did not develop much of an agricultural export economy as the bulk of raw material production was in logging and forest products. The reliance on outside actors for economic decisions for the bulk of Belizean history also means that they have a very low level of entrepreneurship and have had a difficult time developing industrial production on any scale.

A particularly troubling legacy of Belizean history is the long-standing border dispute with Guatemala. Despite the agreements at the time of Belizean independence, many in Guatemala still believe that Belize should be a part of the modern Guatemalan state. In particular, Guatemala argues that the southern half of Belize should be ceded to them. Although this is one of the longest running border disputes in Latin America, it appears that the matter could finally be settled once and for all when the two countries signed an agreement to hold a referendum on the issue in each state to decide the issue.

(Ramos 2015) However, given the longevity of the problem, it is possible that the border dispute could continue indefinitely.

THE BELIZEAN ECONOMY

Despite being a small Central American country, the World Bank classifies Belize as upper middle income with a GDP (PPP) per capita of $8,486 in 2014 which represented a 3.6 percent growth rate over the previous year. Belize has been able to achieve high growth rates and "compared to its Central American counterparts, Belize has been a growth star, starting 1960 as the second-poorest country in the region, but now among the 'top-tier' with a GDP per capita near that of Costa Rica and Panama." (Hausman and Klinger 2007, 3) The World Bank also notes however that poverty has expanded in recent years due to a stagnant economy and a litany of natural disasters. In addition, high debt continues to be a major problem for policy makers. (World Bank) The 2008–2009 global recession hit Belize particularly hard with significant declines in their main exports (citrus and marine products) and a drop off in tourism, particularly overnight tourist stays. In addition, the IMF forecast for long run economic growth is a modest 2.5 percent. (Government of Belize 2012, 5)

Not surprisingly, given the size of the Belizean economy and its limited export goods, Belize has been extremely vulnerable to global economic shocks. This vulnerability to external shocks is enhanced by the traditionally small number of exports, mostly from the agricultural sector. Further exacerbating the narrow band of Belizean exports is the fact that they are primary goods in which Belize has no particularly compelling comparative advantage such as lumber, sugar, mineral fuels, fruit, vegetables, and fish. (IADB 2014, 18) In fact, one of the first major economic shocks after independence occurred in the sugar market during the 1970s and early 1980s and was due in large part to fluctuations in international prices. On the positive side, this incident served as in impetus to expand exports beyond a reliance on sugar, which has been slowly occurring ever since. (Hausman and Klinger 2007, 5)

The national currency, the Belizean dollar, has been pegged to the US dollar at 2:1 since 1976 when it replaced the British Pound. The dollar replaced the pound when the United States passed the United Kingdom as the primary source of Belize's imports and the specific exchange rate was determined by the average level of foreign reserves maintained by the monetary authorities, patterns of foreign exchange inflows and outflows and expectations of future growth in the domestic economy, as well as exports of goods and services. (Metzgen 2012, 13) The main reason that small economies such as Belize will peg their currencies to a larger economy is to "'import' monetary credibility by anchoring to a currency with a credible central bank." (13)

This monetary "credibility" however comes at the expense of monetary flexibility and leaves the Belizean economy even more vulnerable to external shocks. One positive is that Standard & Poor's predicts that the peg will produce price increases of only between 1 percent and 2 percent from 2013–2016. (2013, 3)

In addition, states that depend on tourism get the added benefit of providing cost certainty to incoming tourists who know the exchange rate will not fluctuate. Since a majority of trade and tourists come from the United States, the currency peg can be useful for tourism businesses. In fact, the Belize Tourism Board uses the currency peg and ease of exchange on its tourist website as a selling point for visitors.

> Belize currency exchange is extremely easy for American visitors. The Belize dollar is locked at $2 Belize = $1 USD. So it's very easy to see how much something is costing in USD when you go shopping. Most accommodations and tours are listed in US$ prices, and most restaurants, shops, etc. are listed in BZ$. Nearly everyplace readily accepts USD currency. Most also should accept traveler's checks as long as you write your passport number or driver's license number on the back. Large bills (anything above a $20) are a little more difficult to cash. Shopkeepers generally ask you to spend a minimum amount. ATMs are also available across the country, particularly in most tourist destinations—including Placenica, Punta Gorda, Belmopan, Dangriga, Belize City, San Pedro Ambergris Caye, Caye Caulker, Orange Walk, San Ignacio and Corozal. (Belize Tourism Board)

Not surprisingly, a country's exchange rate is an important factor in determining tourist flows. While the pegged exchange rate will likely help to encourage tourism from the United States, it is also likely to discourage tourism from states whose currency is weak versus the dollar, many of which will find travel to Belize cost prohibitive. This pegged currency system is beneficial for Belize as long as they majority of their tourists are from the United States and they do not have a more expansive export industry and the Belizean dollar's real exchange rate is higher than the pegged rate.

Another economic issue that has risen to prominence in Belize is the birth of an oil industry due to exploration and extraction beginning in 2005 when Belize was able to bring several commercially viable wells into production. Since that time, oil has not only served as an important export, but also as a catalyst for Belize to renegotiate its foreign debt with many of its creditors. This renegotiation was based on the hope that oil exports would spur the economy and that the industry would expand with further discoveries. So far this has not been the case as there have not been any commercially viable deposits discovered since the initial discoveries. Making matters worse, oil production at the existing wells has been in decline over the past few years with no signs of increased production. Despite this, oil is an important export and in 2012 it represented 36 percent of all Belizean exports. (Government of Belize 2012, 7)

Given the mixed results of the Belizean oil industry, with failed exploration and declining production, it is clear that oil extraction is only viable as a short-term economic fix. "The expansion of the oil sector over the last five years has been the single most important factor that has allowed growth to remain mildly positive throughout the crisis; oil output has peaked and is now expected to begin a steady decline." (5) In addition, environmental groups have opposed oil exploration since the very beginning and many find the idea of oil exploration to be in direct opposition to the ability of Belize to cultivate the image needed to become a full-fledged ecotourism destination.

There was also a lot of apprehension in Belize regarding who would receive the oil contracts and how those receiving government largesse would be selected. With the high levels of corruption in the government "these concerns were heightened by the allocation of concessions for oil exploration to multiple small, recently formed domestic companies with little prior experience." (Cisneros-Montemayor et al. 2013, 222) Currently, the only entity engaged in the oil business in Belize is Belize Natural Energy (BNE), which produces "approximately 2,000 barrels of crude oil per day, 1,800 gallons of Liquefied Petroleum Gas (LPG), and 160 thousand cubic feet per day (MCF/D) of fuel gas for electricity generation (internal use)." (Belize Natural Energy) It is forecasted in 2015 that Belize will produce approximately 800,000 barrels of oil, which is about the oil production of 2009. (Government of Belize 2012, 7)

Part of the reason the government had to scramble to find a company that could engage in oil exploration and extraction is the difficulty inherent in starting a business in Belize largely due to corruption and government inefficiency. In the World Bank's Doing Business (DB) report Belize ranks near the bottom not only regionally, but in many areas globally with respect to the ease with which someone can start a business. The numbers below illustrate that these difficulties are present in several facets of starting and running a business in Belize.

These problems can be put into two broad categories: the difficulty in starting a business reflected in the low scores for things like permits, getting credit and electricity, and the difficulty in running a business as reflected in the score for things like paying taxes, trading across borders, and enforcing contracts. In addition, it should be noted that in several categories Belize has actually gotten worse and scores near the bottom of Latin America and the Caribbean, which are their direct competitors. It will be very difficult for Belize to realize its potential for economic growth when the government makes it difficult for someone to start and run a business. The problem of corruption when trying to start a business is so acute that US Department of

Table 3.1. Doing Business in Belize

Activity	*DB 2016 Rank*	*DB 2015 Rank*
Starting a Business	159	149
Dealing with Construction Permits	81	76
Getting Electricity	73	69
Registering Property	128	129
Getting Credit	162	160
Protecting Minority Investors	122	121
Paying Taxes	69	61
Trading Across Borders	117	117
Enforcing Contracts	133	132
Resolving Insolvency	81	82

Source: World Bank Doing Business Rankings, rank out of 189.

State's Investment Climate report warns potential investors that "corruption involved in starting a business in Belize can be troublesome." (2014)

In addition to the widespread corruption in Belize, the government also faces a number of fiscal challenges related to external debt and an expanding budget deficit. Belize has long had debt issues that have been very difficult for them to solve. They were able to successfully restructure their sovereign debt of US$547.5 million in 2013, which provided some relief, however this restructuring only altered Belize's debt payment in the short term as the interest will go from 5 percent to 6.767 percent in August of 2017 and payments on the principal will come due in 2019. (US Department of State 2015, 3) The government of Belize has also been able to make partial payments for its energy needs by utilizing the Venezuelan government's Petro Caribe oil initiative. This is a "loan in which Belize pays Venezuela 50% up front for fuel and repays the rest at 1% interest over 25 years, allowing it to 'hold back' 50% of the cost of fuel to use for other needs." (US Department of State 2015, 3)

It is hoped that the restructuring of Belizean external debt would help to give the government of Belize some "breathing room" and also served as an attempt to halt the cycle of boom and bust that has dogged the country since independence. In a report for the Inter-American Development Bank, Hausman and Klinger refer to this as the "growth syndrome."

> The "growth syndrome" in Belize is that of a highly-indebted state with a crippling debt overhang, arising from periodic public spending binges. This lack of fiscal discipline (whose timing coincides with political cycles) has created the expected symptoms: repeated episodes of growth on the back of

> fiscal expansion with ballooning current account, budget, and trade deficits, which eventually require harsh adjustment and recession. The debt overhang has led to the virtual elimination of public investment, while investments in road maintenance, sanitation, crime, and rural airport upgrading are key for achieving future investment growth. Deficit spending has also led to increases in reserve requirements, and therefore greater taxation on financial intermediation. This, combined with very low aggregate savings and inefficiency in the financial system, has resulted in an extremely high cost of capital in Belize. Although high-potential sectors for investment exist and have been clearly identified, high lending rates and little access to international financial markets have prevented greater investment. (27)

The best way for Belize to structure its economy to use its comparative advantage in sustainable ecotourism and to attract foreign direct investment is to continue with attempts to diversify their export portfolio and prepare the economy for the high probability that oil revenue will decline precipitously or halt altogether in the near future. Given how small the economy of Belize is, it is imperative for the government of Belize to find ways to better integrate into the world economy as capital formation has been a consistent problem area for much of Belize's history. As such, it is of vital importance for Belize to open its economy to the outside world and institute policies that will end corruption and make investment and starting a business there easier. With its rare natural beauty, ecotourism in Belize carries a great deal of potential.

THE DEVELOPMENT OF ECOTOURISM

Despite its obvious potential as a tourism destination, Belize has only recently tried to use tourism (and ecotourism) as a major driving force for economic development. The first real acknowledgement of Belize's potential as a tourist destination came in 1961 when a group of tourism consultants examined the potential of Belize and found that tourism should be a fundamental part of any economic plan for Belize's future. (Morgan and Campbell 1992, 5) This is not surprising given the nature of Belize's possible tourist attractions which combine world-class Caribbean beaches with unique cultural Mayan sites for potential visitors to explore. "The country has great natural and cultural attractions, is conveniently close to the great North American market, and is safe for tourists. The coral reef and cayes offer the finest skin diving, underwater photography, sailing, and fishing in the hemisphere, along with the superlative sun, sea, and sand that visitors to the Caribbean take for granted." (Bolland 1986, 87)

With practically no tourist infrastructure at all in 1961, there was a lot of room for improvement, which the government of Belize sought to remedy via a set of government development initiatives to the industry set out in the

Development Incentive Ordinance of 1960 which provided tax holidays for government-approved tourism enterprises. (Morgan and Campbell 1992, 5) These initiatives did little however to create a Belizean tourism industry and for much of the 1960s and 1970s tourism development was piecemeal with a patchwork of private enterprises creating tourism services on an ad hoc basis with the private sector often taking the lead in tourism development. Given the small Belizean economy and the diffuse nature of the small rural population, this type of development was very difficult and it meant that Belize lacked many of the basic features necessary for tourism. As Morgan and Campbell (1992), researchers at the Central Bank of Belize state:

> The (tourism) industry (in the 1970s) faced numerous problems including: lack of adequate accommodation and complementary facilities; lack of persons with the required skills to serve the industry; the need for improvement in the infrastructure, in particular the airport and major roads; lack of service and entertainment facilities; lack of adequate credit facilities to local businessmen who might be interested in investing in the industry; and a lack of legislation to maintain quality standards in all areas of the industry. (6)

This lack of focus on tourism development was borne of a traditional focus on agricultural export as the central strategy of the Belizean economy going back centuries. Similar to many of their neighbors' reliance on a small band of exports, Belize's reliance on the export of sugar—the price of which fluctuated considerably in the 1980s—motivated Belize to seek out new forms of foreign exchange in much more concrete ways. In this manner the development of tourism in Belize mirrors the development of tourism in Costa Rica as each of them was borne of necessity during an economic crisis as the reliance on a single export proved to be problematic. Evidence of this is the government of Belize declaring tourism the country's second most important industry. (7)

The declaration of tourism as a national priority in 1989 set goals to increase the number of tourists as well as the contribution of tourism to foreign exchange earnings, government revenue, and employment. To do this the government of Belize set out to create a suitable investment climate in tourism services, an expansion of infrastructure, training for individuals in the industry, and a balance between tourism and the environment. This balance is partially facilitated by a focus on ecotourism as well as cultural tourism focusing on the *Ruta Maya*. In addition, the government's plan included preferential treatment for Belizean citizens with the responsibility for investment resting squarely on the private sector. (7–8)

Since the late 1980s, Belize has focused on ecotourism and traditional sun-and-surf tourism, and has become a prominent cruise ship destination. In addition, the government of Belize created the Belize Tourism Board (BTB) with the Belize Tourism Board 1990 Act to oversee the development of the tourism industry. (Belize Tourism Board) One of the BTB's most important responsibilities is to act as the primary marketer of tourism in Belize to the world. In the early days of both the BTB and the Belizean tourism industry, the BTB took full advantage of situating Belize as a new and exotic player in ecotourism vacations by advertising Belize as "Mother Nature's Best Kept Secret." (Hausman and Klinger 2007, 20)

As a result of concerted attempts to boost their tourism industry, by 2010 tourism "emerged as one of the main engines of growth in the Belizean economy and the principal source of foreign exchange. The development of Belize's tourism sector was a targeted government strategy and represents an example of a successful public-private partnership." (Metzgen 2012, 6) The most important attempt by the government of Belize to boost its tourism industry is the National Sustainable Tourism Master Plan for Belize 2030, which is a joint project funded by the government of Belize and the Inter-American Development Bank. The goal of the plan is to grow Belizean tourism "in a manner that is economically, environmentally and socially sustainable." (Government of Belize 2009, 1) The plan has three main goals with two primary components:

> (i) enhancing the tourism experience and resource sustainability at consolidated destinations subject to pressure; (ii) diversifying tourism products in emerging destinations for the overnight market segments; and (iii) strengthening tourism institutions for policy, destination planning, and management. The program consists of two components: Component I: Investments in overnight tourism destinations; and Component II: Institutional strengthening and capacity building for policy, destination planning, and management. (1)

To accomplish these goals, Belize plans to spend approximately US$1.3 billion between 2012 and 2030 on a variety of development projects to improve multiple aspects of their tourism offerings. (3) The goal of many of these projects is to further enhance Belize as an overnight, rather than a cruise excursion destination due to the increased revenue gleaned from eco-tourists who stay in-country for multiple days. As can be seen in Table 3.2, Belize draws far more cruise ship passengers than overnight guests and while Belize's aggregate tourist arrival numbers are not as high as many of its competitors, considering that Belize is a small country with a population of approximately 350,000 people, they draw a lot of tourists for a country of their size.

The attempts by the government of Belize to improve overnight tourist does not mean that they are not also trying to increase the arrival of cruise ship passengers as well. In fact, cruise tourism has increased significantly in Belize.

Table 3.2. Tourist Arrivals to Belize

Year	*Overnight Tourists*	*Cruise Visitors*	*Total Visitors*
2001	195,955	48,116	244,071
2002	199,521	319,690	519,211
2003	220,574	575,196	795,770
2004	230,832	851,436	1,082,268
2005	236,573	800,333	1,036,906
2006	247,309	655,931	903,240
2007	251,422	624,128	875,550
2008	245,007	597,370	842,377
2009	232,249	705,219	937,468
2010	241,919	764,628	1,006,547
2011	250,263	727,878	978,141

Source: Belize Tourism Authority, 2011.

> Cruise tourism has been a rapidly growing segment of the Belize tourism industry. Cruise passenger arrivals grew from 14,183 in 1998 to 597,370 in 2008 or approximately 70.9% of all tourist arrivals. After a marked peak in growth in 2004, the cruise ship segment is showing signs of leveling off with a total of 274 ship calls in 2008, a 32.5% decline in calls relative to the 406 ship calls in 2004, but nearly the same as 2007's 278 ship calls. At the moment, passengers are transported from cruise ships by smaller vessels to the Fort Street Tourism Village in Belize City where they are taken by buses to various nearby destinations. The government is considering the development of a new cruise ship terminal. (Government of Belize 2009, 2–3)

The plan to build a new cruise ship terminal is controversial with many traditional ecotourism operators as well as environmentalists opposed to the idea. One of the main opponents of the cruise terminal is the Belize Tourism Industry Association (BTIA) which states "the environmental damage the cruise port and quantity of persons from the cruise visits would cause to the pristine marine surroundings and the potential economic and natural resources lost is incompatible with long term sustainability and development of Belize's tourism industry." (Belize Tourism Industry Association) The decision between whether the limited resources of the government of Belize should go to increasing cruise passengers or whether it should go to developing resources to encourage sustainable ecotourism is of the utmost importance going forward.

Part of what makes this an important issue is the amount of revenue generated by overnight tourists versus cruise excursionists, with overnight guests representing 88 percent of tourism revenue and 90 percent of revenue when they visit Belize. (Government of Belize 2009, 3) Despite the small percentage of tourism revenue generated by cruise tourism, building the new cruise terminal is one of the top five publicly funded priorities of the National Sustainable Tourism Master Plan for Belize 2030, leaving the development of a handful of mid- to high-end ecolodges to the private sector. (16–19) The government of Belize hopes that high-end (i.e. more expensive) boutique ecolodges will boost the per tourist rate of revenue while limiting the total number of tourists.

Given the ad hoc nature of Belizean tourism development, the expansion of the tourism industry has been mostly local and small scale. In fact the Inter-American Development Bank states that "small enterprises play an unusually large role in Belize's tourism sector, compared with more traditional destinations such as The Bahamas and Barbados." (Rowland, Durante, and Martin 2010, 8–9) One of the best examples of how Belizeans were able to build small-scale ecotourism enterprises from the outset of Belize's ecotourism industry is the Toledo Ecotourism Association (TEA). The TEA was founded in 1990 by a group of Toledo District Maya and Garifuna who wanted to become involved with ecotourism in their local villages. Once formed the group set out to improve their incomes by building a series of small guest houses using their own labor with materials gathered from the surrounding rainforest. One of the most interesting parts of the TEA is how seriously they take giving all participants in the project an equal chance to profit from the arrival of visitors. To accomplish this, when each participating village receives guests, they have to wait their turn before receiving guests again. Similarly, people in the villages who provides things like meals to the ecotourists also take turns in providing services. In this way, the TEA. does everything it can to spread the income from ecotourism to as many people in the participating communities as possible. (Toledo Ecotourism Association)

The Belize Tourism Board also has programs to attract foreigners to live in Belize and specifically targets high-income individuals. As such, the Retired Persons Incentive Act "was designed to benefit retired persons over 45 years of age. To qualify, applicants need proof of income not less than US$2,000 per month through a pension or annuity generated outside of Belize. An approved Qualified Retired Person is allowed to import personal effects and an approved means of transportation free of all customs duties and taxes. All income generated outside of Belize are also free of taxes." (US Department of State 2015, 12)

FOREIGN DIRECT INVESTMENT IN BELIZE

For the most part, Belize is an open economy that allows for foreign ownership of economic enterprises and foreign direct investment is encouraged through a variety of government programs. The two main pieces of legislation that deal with foreign direct investment in Belize are the 1990 International Business Companies Act which allows international investors to engage in "offshore" transactions such as: asset protection and operation of bank accounts, brokerage accounts, ship ownership, and commission arrangements; and the 1992 Trusts Act, which provides for onshore and offshore trusts. (Rowland, Durante, and Martin 2010, 21)

The main government agency that deals with attracting foreign direct investment is the Belize Trade and Investment Development Service (BELTRAIDE). BELTRAIDE solicits investment through three primary mechanisms. The first is an Export Processing Zone (EPZ) which is designed to boost both foreign and domestic investment in export businesses. Companies that are able to benefit from this are treated as being outside national customs territory and enjoy a number of benefits including exemptions from export and import duties and a wide array of taxes including a twenty-year tax holiday which can be extended to deduct losses after the holiday period. (US Department of State 2015, 11)

The second major mechanism used by BELTRAIDE to attract investment is a Commercial Free Zone (CFZ) which is designed to attract investment in the service industry including banking, financial, and insurance services, among others. Services originating in either of the two CFZs can only be sold in Belize and are subject to the usual taxes and duties. The third major mechanism is the International Business Companies Act which is specifically designed to attract offshore companies to Belize. As such, companies that relocate an operation to Belize are not allowed to own property or to conduct any type of business with Belizean citizens. (11)

Like many small economies in the region, Belize via BELTRAIDE "continues to promote foreign direct investment with generous incentives packages coupled with its availability of good land and a resource-abundant natural environment." (3) The problem however is that the government of Belize is often not able to deliver on these promises: investors state that often in practice they do not receive the full extent of the incentives available, that land title is not always reliably secure, and that bureaucratic delays or corruption can be hindrances to starting a business in Belize. There is a sense among investors that incentives can be very beneficial but currently they are administered in an ad hoc manner, with frequent delays or payment not issued as originally guaranteed. (3)

In addition to the difficulty for some investors receiving their promised incentives there are other difficulties for foreign investors including tax issues, domestic ownership rules, and a variety of regulations that sometimes serve to de-incentivize investment in Belize. These include measures that limit foreign control of companies by requiring them to receive clearance from the Belizean Central Bank before being able to invest and protectionist policies that limit competition in some sectors. (4–5) Corruption is also a major problem when attempting to invest in Belize and adds yet another layer of problems to an already often difficult environment for investment or starting a business. The US Department of State (2015) found "potential investors have cited corruption as a barrier to attract foreign direct investments. It is alleged that at times investors were solicited for contributions in return for expedited immigration favors, land acquisition, investment incentives, and exclusive contracts." (3)

These difficulties have created an environment in which foreign direct investment in Belize has been very inconsistent with investment flows stopping and starting based on a range of factors inside the Belizean economy. In fact, early investing booms have played a role in limiting foreign direct investment in the last few years. From 1999 to 2004, Belize experienced a spectacular, externally financed boom; however, the ensuing credit bubble and the cost of replacing storm-damaged infrastructure contributed to a debt overhang and government debt rescheduling in 2007 and 2013. Due to these issues, gross capital formation has lingered near 20 percent of GDP since 2003. (Standard & Poor's 2013, 7) Foreign direct investment numbers are also greatly affected by the government promoting specific industries or projects which results in a large influx of investment over the short term, which then wanes over time. For instance, foreign direct investment in 2012 was nearly double the amount in 2011 when American Sugar Refining bought an 85 percent stake in Belize Sugar Industries Limited for US$60 million which was used for a number of factory improvements to boost efficiency. (8) Table 3.3 illustrates the chaotic nature of foreign direct investment into Belize.

In order to receive a more consistent level of foreign direct investment, Belize needs to find ways to improve the structural issues that negatively affect the economy as well as create a difficult environment for outside investment. This includes greater fiscal discipline and a commitment to improving the efficiency of the government. In 2013, Standard & Poor's graded Belize a B/B- rating but expressed concern regarding high debt and interest burden which creates the vulnerability to external debt shocks. (2) In addition Standard & Poor's goes on to say that despite improvement in some areas of the economy debt and structural problems inhibits economic growth:

> Although tourism receipts and foreign direct investment (FDI) in the agricultural and tourism sectors picked up this year, we expect growth to remain below historical norms at 2.5% on average over 2014–2016. The country's debt

Table 3.3. Foreign Direct Investment to Belize

Year	FDI inflows to Belize in USD Millions
2002	25.4
2003	-10.9
2004	111.5
2005	126.9
2006	108.8
2007	140.4
2008	169.7
2009	108.8
2010	97.2
2011	93.8
2012	194.2

Source: World Bank.

> overhang, its economic structure intensive in primary goods exports, and the less favorable external financing environment for FDI over the past five years have constrained Belize's growth below historical rates and those of peers. (2)

The problem of Belize's debt overhang means that it is imperative to grow the economy via foreign direct investment and to maintain fiscal discipline. The dual problems of high debt and low growth create a cycle that is often difficult for any economy to solve, especially one that is as small as Belize. The best way for Belize to increase economic growth and lower external debt is build an economy that creates the factors that will lead to sustainable ecotourism and foreign direct investment.

FACTORS THAT ENABLE SUSTAINABLE ECOTOURISM AND FOREIGN DIRECT INVESTMENT

One of the most important factors that will negatively affect tourism and foreign investment is an unstable government and a legal system that does not respect the rule of law. While Belize has been a democracy since its independence in 1981, it has been long been plagued by a high crime rate as well as a significant amount of government corruption—so significant that it interferes with almost all aspects of public life in Belize. The extent of corruption in Belize is difficult to know as the country has not participated in Transparency International's Corruption Perception Index since ranking 109th out of 180 countries in 2008. (Ramos 2014) While Belize has a number of anticorruption laws on the books, they are rarely enforced. One of the best examples of the failure of Belizean anticorruption laws is the Prevention of Corruption in Public Life Act which was passed in 1994 and was meant to be a comprehensive approach to end, or at least curtail, corruption by public officials. When the law was passed it established an Integrity Commission which was responsible for monitoring the declarations of the assets and finances of all public officials. The law gives the Commission wide-ranging powers to investigate officials at virtually all levels of government and explicitly criminalizes corruption. The offenses included are the use of office for private gain, code of conduct breaches, the use of public funds for private gain, as well as bribery. Punishment for violations of the law may include a fine of up to US$5,000, severe reprimand, forfeiture of property acquired by corruption, and removal from office. The last report of the integrity commission was published in 2005 and no cases under this act have ever led to prosecution. (US Department of State 2015, 18)

Despite these and other problems such as unemployment, drug trafficking, and a high level of street crime, Belize has been able to establish itself as a consolidated functioning democracy. In fact, it rates a score of 8 out of 10 on Country Watch's Political Risk Index, placing it near the top of Latin America and the Caribbean as a country with very little political risk. (Country Watch 2015, 14) Each of these issues present substantial problems for economic development, particularly in attracting ecotourists and foreign direct investment. "Belize has many natural attractions, a favorable exchange rate, and proximity to the USA. It is attempting to capitalize on these attributes by marketing itself as a tourist destination. However, Belize is also beset with a very high crime rate—a function of a myriad of social, political, and economic problems." (Hanson, Warchol, and Zupan 2004, 241) These problems include an unemployment rate of 10.1 percent and a poverty rate of 41.3. (Statistical Institute of Belize)

Although it is not likely to be of comfort to potential ecotourists thinking of traveling to Belize, the United States Department of State Bureau of Diplomatic Security states that even though Belize's crime rate is high the "the majority of crimes are burglaries and thefts, often without injuries" (United States Department of State Bureau of Diplomatic Security 2015), rather than the violent crime that has plagued many parts of Latin America throughout its history. Much of the crime problem in Belize stems from high unemployment, street crime, and drug trafficking. Although Belize's crime rate makes the tourism industry nervous, for the most part crime in Belize is centered on the two major cities, Belmopan and Belize City—neither of which attracts large numbers of visitors.

Belize's significant problem with drug trafficking is even more troubling given the porous border with Guatemala which serves as a major shipment point for illegal drugs destined for the United States. More troubling still is the role of Belizean officials in the drug trade. The US Bureau for International Narcotics and Law Enforcement Affairs stated that the ability of the government of Belize to combat trafficking was severely undermined by deeply entrenched corruption which reached into senior levels of government. (Duffy 2000, 556) Despite these issues, Belize has very little political violence, with instances usually centered on domestic Belizean political issues.

Given the importance of low crime and the rule of law in order to attract foreign ecotourists as well foreign direct investment, it is imperative that Belize address problems of crime and corruption so it can better develop sustainable ecotourism. Exacerbating the problems of crime and drug trafficking is a police force that is severely underfunded and in many ways barely able to do its job.

> (Belize is) plagued by a poorly funded police department, high crime rates, and slow economic growth. While exhibiting modern organization, training, and ideas, the major hindrance to the Belize National Police is a lack of adequate funding which in turn manifests itself in a severe lack of basic resources for crime control, investigations, and service provision. This in turn leads to low morale among officers and a lack of confidence by the public, fostered in part by the media and a resulting increased fear of crime which harms its developing tourism industry. The Belize Police have responded with a variety of innovations to overcome these difficulties, yet most mainly represent stop-gap measures. (Hanson, Warchol, and Zupan 2004, 255)

It also appears that Belize's reaction to the 2008–2009 global recession had a negative effect on the rule of law, which in turn had a negative effect on foreign direct investment. "Since 2008, the global economic downturn, the nationalization of the major telecommunications and electricity companies, continued high import tariffs, and new legislation on arbitration paralleled a decrease in the flow of foreign direct investment." (US Department of State 2015, 3) The association between a panicked response to the recession and a move away from an open economy in which the state nationalizes some industries is unfortunately not particularly surprising given the government of Belize's proclivity for regulation. Belize's reaction to economic downturn also partially explains the desire to build a new cruise terminal and sign long-term contracts with cruise lines to bring passengers since these contracts represent a steady source of income.

The nationalization of the telecommunications and electric companies is particularly problematic for attracting foreign investment and despite the Belizean constitution containing explicit statements describing a strong right to private property, private property rights in Belize are not always absolute. The combination of the nationalization of foreign-owned companies and the high rate of government corruption is a toxic mix for many investors that could create a sharp drop off in outside investment similar to the declines in Venezuela and Argentina when they nationalized foreign-owned industries. If the government of Belize were to appropriate land or other private property for public use under a legitimate system of eminent domain with equitable compensation, it would be unpopular. Despite being unpopular, if appropriation of private assets were rare, it would not necessarily have a large effect of foreign direct investment to Belize. The problem in Belize is that too often the government appropriates private property for personal or political gain. (7) As such, this sort of appropriation of private property will have a long-term deleterious effect on outside investment. Making matters worse still, compensation for investors in expropriated businesses in many sectors such as the telecommunications and electric companies discussed above have never been compensated.

In addition to problems related to expropriation, Belize, like many of its neighbors, has a very poor land deed system in which absolute ownership of a parcel of land is often very difficult to ascertain. These problems stem from not only disorganization and inefficiency in the government of Belize, but unsurprisingly is also often due to corruption. "Numerous landowners, including several U.S. citizens, have been victims of land fraud, where title documents were transferred out of their possession without their knowledge, and in most cases the owners have not received compensation. There have been public allegations that government officials have been complicit in some of the fraud." (13) Obviously, investors want to be certain that when they purchase a parcel of land, the person selling it rightfully owns it and is entitled to sell it.

Another long-term problem in Belize is the difficulties in building and maintaining a modern infrastructure. Part of the problem stems from Belize's low population density which makes roads connecting places in which very few people live highly problematic. In order to attract ecotourists as well as foreign direct investment Belize needs to improve its infrastructure, which is particularly poor in rural areas.

> An extensive construction program funded by the government, starting in the early 1980s, as well as improvement projects funded by international aid, have led to significant improvements in the road network. Paved highways connect most major urban settlements and border areas. However, the situation is difficult in rural areas, where many roads remain unpaved or have gravel or marl surfaces. Compared with other countries in the region, Belize has a low percentage of roads paved to total roads: 17 percent. Jamaica has 70 percent paved, but Costa Rica has only 22 percent. (Rowland, Durante, and Martin 2010, 34)

The infrastructure problems in Belize are another major area for improvement discussed in the National Sustainable Tourism Master Plan for Belize

2030 and there are plans to improve several different infrastructure areas including roads, ports, and the building of a new airport.

Another area that figures prominently in the government's plan is education. Given the small population in Belize, the country has often experienced shortages of skilled personnel across a number of economic activities. This shortage creates many problems for attracting foreign direct investment and ecotourists since both industries require workers with a high level of expertise. As Standard & Poor's (2013) points out "a shortage of skilled labor limits [Belize's] capacity to attract investment in manufacturing or business services." (6) Many of these problems begin early in a child's education as the Belizean educational system is uneven and suffers from problems of access, particularly among poor and marginalized communities. Writing for the Inter-American Development Bank, Näslund-Hadley, Alonzo, and Martin give a dire warning regarding the status of education in Belize.

> Belize is paying a lot for education but getting little. More youth are outside the school system than in it and many fail to make the transition to the workforce. More and more youth drop out of school and become involved in gang activities. Action is needed if Belize is not to lose a whole generation of youth. This document discusses the current situation of the Belizean education sector and its progress over the last 10 years, its relative performance compared with other countries in the region, and the policies currently being implemented by the education sector in Belize. While the challenges are great, the recommendation is to focus on increased efficiency, quality and equity. (2013, 3)

The interesting part of Belize's failures in education policy is that unlike many of its neighbors, the problems do not necessarily stem from problems of funding. Instead, the main problems stem from the structure of the education system and the need for skilled teachers at virtually every level. As such the Inter-American Development Bank advocates for a series of five interventions to improve the public school system in Belize, there are:

1. Establish high student learning expectations to guide the provision and monitoring of education services to all levels
2. Ensure that new students start school ready to learn
3. Provide effective teachers to all students
4. Help schools use resources more effectively to allow more children to learn
5. Support more youth to complete vocational and tertiary education making them prepared to contribute to society. (Näslund-Hadley, Alonzo, and Martin 2013, 33–35)

The good news is that the government of Belize has made major investments in public education over the last decade meaning that these reforms are possible without increasing the amount of funding. For most of their history Belize has been a highly insular society, an attribute that must change in order for Belizeans to value education and compete in a globalized world. In addition, Belize must improve access to education to ensure that students from across the economic spectrum are able to participate in the economy.

COMPARATIVE ADVANTAGES AND FUTURE PROSPECTS

The most obvious comparative advantage for sustainable ecotourism in Belize is the combination of Caribbean beaches and distinctive Mayan cultural tourism sites. In addition, Belize still has a mostly "off-the-beaten-path" reputation, especially for those who want to visit for a multiday ecotourism trip rather than just part of a day via a cruise. The most interesting comparative advantage for Belize is, as an English speaking country, its attractiveness to many tourists from the United States and Canada.

Belize also has another distinct comparative advantage based on the fact that its primary markets are in the United States and Canada. With all its ecotourism focused on the Caribbean rather than on the Pacific side of Central America, Belize a shorter trip from the eastern seaboard of the United States and Canada. This helps to situate Belize as a Caribbean location which will allow it to compete with its Central American neighbors in addition to island destinations in the Caribbean. In a report prepared for the Central Bank of Belize, Metzgen (2012) writes:

> There are also many opportunities for growth in sustainable ecotourism and cultural tourism due to the Mayan archaeological sites of Belize. Further diversifying Belize's tourism product, as planned, to emphasize its comparative advantage in ecotourism based on Belize's rainforest and Mayan heritage would also be important. Belize is among just a handful of countries with Mayan historical sites as Belize was once the center of the Mayan Empire. Ecotourism is also a growing industry for Belize and helps to support conservation initiatives consistent with Horizon 2030 vision. (19)

In order for Belize to fully develop its tourism industry as well as attract foreign direct investment, the government must do something to curtail the corruption across a variety of institutions, In addition, it is imperative for the government of Belize to break down the barriers to starting a business. Particularly concerning is the inability of small- and medium-scale entrepreneurs to easily start and maintain a business. This is especially important given that "private investment in small hotels and tourism operators has increased." (Standard & Poor's 2013, 7) The tradition of Belizean ecotourism as small-scale is one of the most important factors for the country to develop a tourism industry that fits the model of sustainable ecotourism. In addition, this also means that the government of Belize must also not give in to the temptation to expand their presence in cruise ship tourism as cruise lines put a lot of pressure on the natural environment and provide only a modest amount of Belizean tourism revenue. Thankfully, there is some evidence that there is a policy shift away from resort-style and cruise ship tourism and toward more small-scale sustainable ecotourism. As Cisneros-Montemayor et al. (2013) point out:

> There have been concerted efforts to improve tourism management in the country, both by the government and by non-governmental organizations and the private sector. An important aspect has been the tendency to shift away from traditional "mass consumption" sites towards smaller-scale ecotourism initiatives that promote the conservation of nature, yet still provide economic and social benefits to mitigate the effects of restricted access to resources. (221)

A lot of the future of the economy will be determined by the extent to which Belizeans embrace globalization and use their unique comparative advantages to attract ecotourists. In order to do this they must embrace the tenets of neoliberalism and open their economy to the outside world as fully as possible. Due to the similarities between Belize and Costa Rica, the Costa Rican example is particularly instructive to Belizean ecotourism. In some ways, Costa Rica serves as a cautionary tale given that many of the same forces that have encouraged Costa Rican policy makers to shift focus from small-scale ecotourism to more mainstream cruise and resort tourism.

In order to build a coherent long-term ecotourism industry it is necessary for the government of Belize to fully engage all stakeholders, particularly local populations. One of the strengths of Belizean ecotourism has traditionally been the involvement of local stakeholders in an industry that has long been focused on small operations. According to Alexander and Whitehouse "the key to whether any tourism development is sustainable lies in one of the basic premises of Belize's responsible tourism mandate, that is, the promotion of local participation in decision-making processes." (2004, 140) While the Belizean government needs to fully embrace the opportunities presented by sustainable ecotourism, it needs to do so in a way that minimizes economic leakage by fulfilling its own mandate to create a small-scale and sustainable industry.

Chapter Four

Panama: Ecotourism and the Canal

Situated on a prime spot connecting the world's two major oceans, Panama's history has been dominated by its strategic position. Starting during the colonial period, Panamanian development has often been secondary to major powers using the isthmus as a shipping point for their own benefit. The dreams of an isthmian canal and its ultimate construction and administration dominates Panamanian history. Panama's geographical importance also means that it is the "the Latin American country most heavily influenced and shaped by the United States over the long term." (Harding 2006, 1)

Panama's history and geography also mean that it is uniquely situated to benefit from policies that encourage the development of sustainable ecotourism and open the economy to foreign direct investment. Panama is among the most open economies in the Americas and has long benefitted from engagement with the outside world. In addition, it has a number of natural attractions that can serve as a basis for an ecotourism industry. Its historical relationship with the United States also gives it an advantage over other destinations when trying to attract US tourists. All of these factors together mean that Panama could benefit greatly from a set of policies that encourages growth in each of these areas.

PRECOLONIAL PANAMA

Similarly to other countries in pre-Columbian Latin America, Panama had a large and diverse indigenous population pre-conquest numbering between 500,000 and 750,000 people among sixty different tribal groups. (Knippers Black and Flores 1989, 6) In addition, the importance of Panama as a transit point was established long before Europeans arrived and there is evidence that people living in Panama used the isthmus to transport goods and people as early as 12,000 BC (Harding 2006, 11) Panama's unique geographical position also means that it has long been influenced by Central and South America as well as the Caribbean, including many of the indigenous groups of Panama that share a number of characteristics with groups from other parts of Central America or from what is now Colombia. In addition to Panama's strategic location, Europeans would find themselves interested in the many gold items the indigenous population used as decorations and in religious ceremonies. This would prompt Christopher Columbus in 1502 to report back to Spain that the native peoples of Panama had gold in abundance (12) which further encouraged the Spanish to send more conquistadores.

SPANISH COLONIALISM IN PANAMA

The first European to explore Panama was Spanish explorer Rodrigo de Bastidas who was looking for sources of gold in 1501. This was quickly followed by the establishment of a short-lived settlement founded by Christopher Columbus in 1503. In 1513 Vasco Nunez de Balboa made a "discovery" that would dominate Panama's role within Spanish colonialism, when he confirmed that the narrow isthmus of Central America, did in fact, connect the Atlantic to the Pacific Ocean. This fact led to the creation of the *Camino Real* (Royal Road) across Panama which transported massive amounts of New World gold to galleons bound for Spain and served as an early version of the Panama Canal. "In addition to its importance for the Spanish colonial empire and global trade, the *Camino Real* had a lasting mark on Panamanian history and molded the formation of the Panamanian economy, population and culture." (Strassnig 2010, 159)

Due to its strategic location, the King of Spain decreed in1538 that all Spanish territory from Nicaragua to Cape Horn was to be administered by the *audencia* in Panama, a situation that lasted until 1543 when the difficulties of administrating such a large area became apparent and by 1567 Panama was attached to the Viceroyalty of Perú. (Knippers Black and Flores 1989, 10) Panama's administration by the Viceroy in Perú was indicative of Spain's desire to accumulate as much gold as possible and send it back to Spain and of the importance of Panama as a transit point. Since Spanish ships could not navigate around the cape of Africa until the seventeenth century, everything and everyone that passed from the colonies back to Spain made the overland journey through Panama (Gallup-Díaz 2010, 419)

Despite its strategic economic position, Panama's fortunes as the major shipping point for goods to Spain were mixed. While a great deal of the gold, and later silver, acquired by the Spaniards in the colonies passed through it, Panama added very little to its distribution or loading. In addition, there was very little domestic production and Spain discouraged the production of finished goods and foreign trade unless the goods passed through Spain. (Knippers Black and Flores 1989, 10–11) This does not mean that there were no benefits for Panama, however the vast majority of benefits were concentrated in Panama City, so much so that "by 1670, Panama City was the wealthiest city in the New World." (Harding 2006, 13). This pattern of development in which Panama City enjoys the vast majority of the benefits of transisthmusian trade is something that continues to this day.

The use of Panama as a transit point for goods to Spain and the wealth of Panama City did not go unnoticed by buccaneer Henry Morgan, who, along with 1,400 men, defeated the Spanish garrison and looted the city in 1671. In the battle with Morgan and the subsequent looting, Panama City was destroyed by fire and rebuilt two years later. (Knippers Black and Flores 1989, 12) Much of the conflict between Spain and numerous groups of Caribbean pirates was not a localized series of events, but was instead due to intra-European rivalries being played out in the New World. Piracy in the Caribbean would however play an important role in Panama's economic well-being because "the gold wealth that had attracted the pirates [made] the Caribbean so dangerous that Spanish ships began to opt for the longer but safer route around South America from Perú's gold mines." (Harding 2006, 14) The alteration of the route away from Panama and instead from Perú to Spain fundamentally altered the viability of Panama as a colony and greatly diminished its importance. The final blow occurred in 1739 when "a British fleet destroyed the port of Porto Bello and Spain finally removed Panama's trading privileges. Panama's autonomy was withdrawn and from 1740 to 1821 the isthmus became a forgotten backwater area." (14) Panama would thus go from backwater to prominence, then to being relatively unimportant backwater to Spanish colonialism once again.

INDEPENDENCE AND GRAN COLOMBIA

In many ways, Panama's status as a backwater helped it to avoid the violence and bloodshed that accompanied independence from Spain in other parts of Spanish America. Even as Panama receded into the background of Spain's overseas possessions, the idea for a canal across the isthmus never died. In fact, the idea for a canal often combined with a burgeoning Latin American, as well as Panamanian, nationalism in which many were willing to invite a foreign power to overthrow Spain and create a canal. By the mid-eighteenth century, many in Spanish America believed that a revolution was imminent due to the greatly weakened status of Spain and the continuing animosity between *peninsulares*, Spaniards born in Spain and sent to the colonies to govern, and *criollos*, the traditional colonial elite of Spanish descent. In addition, *criollos* in the Viceroyalty of New Granada, many of whom dreamed of independence, also knew that Panama would be a key economic and strategic point in any newly formed state or states. Early candidates for foreign intervention in order to build a canal across Panama included France, the United States, and Great Britain. "In 1787, future revolutionary leader Francisco Miranda of Venezuela 'invited' Britain to invade the isthmus in exchange for financial assistance for the imminent revolution against Spain." (15)

Finally, in 1821 Panama, along with the Viceroyalty of New Granada, declared its independence from Spain and joined with Simon Bolívar's grand project to unite postcolonial Latin America, known as Gran Colombia, which encompassed the modern-day countries of Colombia, Venezuela, Bolivia, Ecuador, and Perú. Bolivar's dream was not to reconstitute Spanish colonialism, but instead to set out on a path in which Gran Colombia would be the guarantor of liberty in South America, the platform for the struggle for independence and for the creation of the new states. (de la Reza 2013, 11) This relationship was short-lived and in 1830 Colombia pulled out of the confederation, taking its province of Panama with it.

Despite Panama's history as a colony of Spain, a part of the Viceroyalty of New Granada, a part of Gran Colombia and then a province of Colombia, Panama was still able to cultivate an increasingly strong Panamanian nationalism separate and distinct from its place as parts of other countries and empires. Panamanian nationalism was based on its unique ethnic makeup, geography, its place in various political arrangements, and the idea that economic viability was possible if they could negotiate with an outside power to build a canal without the interference of Colombia. Starting almost immediately after the breakup of Gran Colombia and the integration into Colombia, Panamanian leaders attempted to break free from Colombia. The most successful of these early rebellions occurred in 1840 when Panamanian rebels were able to capitalize on an internal conflict within Colombia and briefly win their independence, only to be reintegrated the following year. (Harding 2006, 16) Unlike many of the conflicts that arose in Latin America in the period directly after independence from Spain, Panama's rebellion was not centered on the conflict between conservatives and liberals, but rather on Panama creating its own path and economic development based on the need for a canal. Méndez (1980) argues that "the leaders of the 1840 rebellion, far from being wildly revolutionary, were instead bent on ameliorating conditions in Panama by achieving economic development, or at least a more beneficial utilization of the region's geographic and economic assets." (270)

PANAMA, THE UNITED STATES AND THE CANAL

As the power of the United States grew and the power of many European states receded during the nineteenth century, the United States began to look for ways to press their advantage and one of the best ways to do so was to finally build a canal across the isthmus. In 1846 Panama and the United States signed the Bidlack-Mallarino Treaty which would forever change the relationship between the two countries. The treaty removed the existing restrictive tariffs on US goods, gave US citizens and goods the right of free transit across Panama as well as gave the United States the right to intervene to maintain social and political stability while also confirming the neutrality of the isthmus and Colombia's sovereignty over it. (Knippers Black and Flores 1989, 18)

The Bidlack-Mallarino Treaty also led to the construction of a rail line across Panama, the goal of which was to speed up the transit of people, goods, and mail to California. The rail line became even more important as people started to pour into California due to the gold rush. The construction of the railroad is also a key ingredient to the social makeup of Panama since very few Panamanians worked on its construction, this led to the importation of laborers from the West Indies, Africa, China, and Europe. (Harding 2006, 19) Despite the economic benefit derived from the new railroad, its completion served to ramp up Panamanian nationalism as both foreign capital and foreign visitors increased tremendously. Panamanians had long been dictated to by outside forces and the construction of the Panama Railroad helped to exacerbate the tensions between Panama and outsiders, particularly the United States. These tensions were further aggravated by the type of American that was traversing the railroad in the mid-nineteenth century, many on their way to California to "make it big" in the gold rush. This included "many unsavory types, who according to contemporary accounts, were little more than criminals. All too often, they passed their time drunk while waiting for ships." (21)

The success of the Panama Railroad also served to illustrate just how much money could be made via travel across Panama. Almost immediately the railroad was a huge success with profits in the first year of over US$7 million; stock dividends went from 15 to 44 percent and for a time was the highest stock price on the New York Stock Exchange. (McCullough 1977, 35–36) With the growth in Panamanian nationalism throughout the period, the economic success which motivated the major powers to build a canal served to further imbue Panamanians with nationalism as yet again they were mostly locked out of the economic benefits of the railroad.

Despite the influence of the United States, it was France that first attempted to build a canal in 1880, a venture that ended in financial disaster in 1889. France's problems with building the canal stemmed not only from the difficulty of the excavation work, but from disease which greatly affected those working on the canal. Despite France's inability to complete the canal, they completed approximately two-thirds of the necessary excavation for the project. (Knippers Black and Flores 1989, 20) When the French attempt to build the canal failed, it appeared as though a canal through Panama might never be built.

The eventual construction of the canal was based on three main factors. First, the French attempt had accomplished a great deal of the digging and had employed so many workers that many of them remained to work on the United States' attempt. Second, the Spanish-American War of 1898 left the United States with overseas territories and the need to project power on a much more global scale. Third, Panamanian tensions with Colombia had finally reached the breaking point, which gave the United States the perfect opportunity to deal directly with the Panamanians and exact a deal that would give the United States control over the canal in exchange for their help in breaking with Colombia. These events provided the opportunity that both the United States and Panama had long waited for and the canal was soon to be a reality. As Harding (2006) points out, "With Colombia in disarray, Panamanians on the verge of revolt, and Roosevelt's administration eager for rights to finish the canal, a hurricane of opportunity was forming of the isthmus." (30)

In November of 1903 with the help of the United States military, Panama finally gained its independence from Colombia. Only five days after Panama declared its independence, Panamanian diplomatic representative to the United States Philippe Bunau-Varilla concluded the Isthmian Canal Convention with US Secretary of State John Hay. Bunau-Varilla, who had not lived in Panama for seventeen years, had purchased his position as diplomatic representative from the Panamanian rebels, also wrote the Panamanian declaration of independence and constitution and designed the Panamanian flag all from his room in the Waldorf-Astoria in New York City. (Knippers Black 1989, 23) The speed of the agreement between the United States and a Frenchman representing Panamanian interests angered Panamanian nationalists and would set a negative tone for US-Panamanian relations that exists to this day. Panamanians were further angered by the content of the agreement that Bunau-Varilla made with the United States on behalf of Panama which gave the United States extensive rights to the Panama Canal. These rights included "[the] grant 'in perpetuity of the use, occupation, and control' of a sixteen kilometer-wide strip of territory and extensions of three nautical miles into the sea from each terminal 'for the construction, maintenance, operation, sanitation, and protection' of an isthmian canal." (23)

When the United States began construction of the canal in late 1904, the first order of business was to control the diseases—particularly malaria and yellow fever—that had ravaged the previous attempt at a canal. Through the eradication of mosquitoes and the construction of clean water and sanitation systems, it is estimated that around 71,000 lives and 40 million days of sickness were saved. The second major difficulty faced by the canal builders was digging the canal through Panama's varied terrain, in particular its mountains. Despite these difficulties, nearly ten years after it was begun on August 15, 1914, the Panama Canal had its first complete passage. (26)

The construction of the canal did not, however, serve to lessen Panamanian angst over US domination and US-Panamanian relations were dominated by the canal. Many Panamanian nationalists were unhappy with the deal given to the United States in the Canal Treaty and once again saw others benefitting from Panama's geographic position.

> Given no property rights, Panama has been forced in the past to accept reluctantly any residual relationship defined by the United States. As a result of Panama's inability to set rates and obtain revenue sharing arrangements indeed, being prohibited from any control over the territory leased to the United States—a substantial subsidy to world shipping interests has resulted, along with lower prices to the consumers in countries of cargo destination. (Osborne 1977, 511)

The construction of a canal, long the dream of many Panamanians had come to fruition, but its major positive benefits were being felt elsewhere.

This fact meant that tensions between the United States and Panama were always just under the surface with rebellions and uprisings among Panamanians frequent. Throughout the time the United States controlled the canal they enacted numerous minor reforms, but none that would totally placate Panamanian nationalists. Similarly to the manner in the Spanish-American War helped US policy makers to understand their need for a transoceanic canal, the Great Depression and the rise Fascism and Nazism made them understand that they could not continue with the status quo in their relations with Panama and that their policies were exacerbating nationalists movements not just in Panama, but across Latin America.

> In the late 1920s, United States policymakers noted that nationalist aspirations in Latin America were not producing desired results. United States occupation of the Dominican Republic, Haiti and Nicaragua had not spawned exemplary political systems nor had widespread intervention resulted in a receptive attitude toward United States trade and investments. As the subversive activities of Latin American Nazi and Fascist sympathizers gained momentum in the 1930s, the United States became concerned about the need for hemispheric solidarity. (Knippers Black 1989, 29)

The result of this concern for the impact of US policy on Latin America was the so-called Good Neighbor Policy enacted by President Franklin D. Roosevelt in 1933. In it Roosevelt promised to adhere to policies of nonintervention and not to interfere in the domestic affairs of Latin American states. Given the huge US interest in the Panama Canal, this would prove to be a tall order and was exacerbated by the election of Arnulfo Arias as president of Panama in 1938 on a staunchly nationalist platform. Arias rode to the presidency at the head of a "mass movement known as Panameñismo. Its essence was nationalism, which in Panama's situation meant opposition to United States hegemony. Arias aspired to rid the country of non-Hispanics, which meant not only North Americans, but also West Indians, Chinese, Hindus and Jews." (32)

While Arias certainly appealed to the most hardcore nationalists, his message also found success in the Panamanian middle class whose nationalist resentment had been exacerbated by the suffering of the Great Depression. He was ultimately undone by his allegiance to Nazi Germany and his own heavy-handed government. "In addition to the carrot of nationalism that he offered to the public, Arias also wielded an equally effective stick. To tighten his grip on power, he utilized authoritarian measures such as jailing dissidents, subverting newspapers, and disenfranchising Panama's non-Spanish speaking population." (Harding 2006, 41) Had Arias been a more run-of-the-mill right-wing dictator, he likely would not have drawn the attention of the United States and could have actually drawn their support; Arias' support for Nazi Germany would be his ultimate undoing. In the end Arias' admiration and even allegiance to the Nazis encouraged the United States to forget the Good Neighbor Policy and resume a policy of intervention in Panama to ensure that they had unfettered access to the canal and Arias was ultimately deposed in a coup in 1941. (41–2) Despite being deposed in 1941, Arias dominated Panamanian politics for much of the mid-twentieth century and was president from 1940 to 1941, 1949 to 1951, and for eleven days in 1968. Arias never finished a term and was deposed by the military each time and many believe he should have been the winner in two additional elections (1964 and 1984) but lost due to electoral fraud. (Knippers Black 1989, 32)

Throughout the 1950s and 1960s, the dominant theme of US-Panamanian relations was finding a way to renegotiate the Canal Treaty and the period was punctuated by several uprisings, the most of which occurred in 1964 and was a dispute about flying the Panamanian flag in the Canal Zone. (38) The 1964 riots served to catalyze Panamanian nationalists into a final push for sovereignty over the canal. The final step was the emergence of Omar Torrijos as Panama's military dictator after being part of a *junta* that deposed Arias in 1968. Torrijos was something different for Panama as "Never before has modern Panama endured a military dictatorship, and Torrijos was unique both as Panama's first military strongman and as the first Latin American leader since Fidel Castro to stand resolutely against the US hegemony in Latin America." (Harding 2006, 68)

Since its construction, many Panamanians had longed to renegotiate the Canal Treaty and hoped to one day achieve full sovereignty over the Canal Zone and Omar Torrijos was just the leader to do it. While never the official president of Panama, from 1968 to 1981 all major decisions in Panama were made by him. Torrijos would presage Latin American leaders such as Hugo Chavez and actively befriended enemies of the United States like Fidel Castro and Momar Qadhafi. (69) Torrijos used the court of public opinion and often turned to international bodies to drum up support for Panamanian control of the canal. He was also not averse to threats of destroying the canal or US interests in the Canal Zone. By the late 1970s it became apparent that some sort of compromise was necessary and Osborne (1977) argued that "a more equitable and reasonable arrangement is required to avert any potential violence or damage to the Canal and to avoid any further erosion in US–Latin American relations. In a political and diplomatic sense, the lack of a timely agreement could prove costly to the United States." (519) With this in mind, President Jimmy Carter negotiated a treaty in 1977 in which the United States would turn over the canal to the Republic of Panama by the year 2000. Though widely unpopular at home, Carter turned the Canal over to Panama not only to smooth over relations with Panama specifically and Latin America generally, but the Canal had become outdated and could not accommodate large modern ships without a costly expansion.

MANUEL NORIEGA

When Omar Torrijos died in a place crash in 1981 his death left a major power vacuum in Panamanian politics and four generals vied for control of the country, one of them was Manuel Noriega who had been head of intelligence under Torrijos. (Harding 2006, 92) By 1983 the US-trained CIA informant Noriega was in effective control of Panama. While Torrijos and Noriega shared a number of characteristics, Noriega's worldview was not based on nationalism, but instead his own self-enrichment. Noriega was also quite willing to do whatever it took to preserve his power and income that resulted.

> Noriega ruled Panama because he and his co-thugs controlled the guns, rockets, mortar, truncheons and tear gas. Any citizen who defied Noriega by rational argument risked being answered by bullets. Jails were used to hold political prisoners—citizens who disagreed too loudly with Noriega. Somehow, miraculously, there was an election in May 1989, and Noriega's candidate was defeated. No matter; Noriega had the power. The opposition candidates appealed to reason, to fairness, to the will of the people; Noriega invoked the logic of brute force, of steel, of gunpowder, of the infliction of imprisonment and disappearance. The electoral victors were crushed. (D'Amato 1990, 517)

While Noriega was known in Washington, DC, and his ascendency to power was welcomed by many in Washington, by the late 1980s the relationship between Noriega and the United States broke down amid the violence and uncertainty in Panama. With the United States scheduled to turn over the canal to Panama on December 31, 1999, it was imperative that there be political stability. The first step in removing Noriega from power included two indictments against him in the US Federal Court in Miami on charges of drug trafficking and money laundering. With Panama's economy in shambles and the violence of Noriega, it was hoped that Noriega would be removed from power without foreign intervention and that the indictments would push the anti-Noriega forces in Panama to action. "The Reagan and Bush Administrations hoped for and preferred a Panamanian solution to end Noriega's rule, such as a coup d'etat or a popular uprising of the kind that removed from power dictators like Anastasio Somozo of Nicaragua or Ferdinand Marcos of the Philippines." (Harding 2006, 108) When no uprising against Noriega was successful, on December 20, 1989, US President George H. W. Bush ordered an invasion of Panama to remove him. Despite the economic damage to many homes and businesses in Panama, a CBS News poll found that 80 percent of Panamanians, even those who had lost homes or family members approved of the invasion. A similar number did not want the United States to give up the canal due to fears of politicians using the revenue from the canal for cronyism. (116)

Since Noriega had annulled the May 1989 presidential election, the US invasion allowed the election winner, Guillermo Endara, to be sworn into office. Given over two decades of military rule, Endara had a difficult road ahead of him because so many areas of Panamanian public life needed reform due to over two decades of military government, the interventions of the United States and myriad economic, political, and social problems which were not solved just because Noriega was removed. Nevertheless, "President Endara was able to solve some of Panama's immediate problems and during his term, President Endara made great progress in restoring functioning political institutions after 21 years of military-controlled government, and under his administration, a new civilian Public Force replaced Noriega's Panama Defense Forces." (Sullivan 2012, 3)

President Endara's major problems in governing Panama were a lack of legitimacy and the idea among Panamanians that he was installed by the United States. While Endara had won the 1989 election the night before the invasion Endara and his two vice-presidents were invited to dinner at a US military base and were told that an invasion was imminent. Faced with the choice between having the United States install him or form an occupation government, Endara and his two vice-presidents were sworn into office by US military officers on a US military base. (Harding 2006, 114) President Endara's issues of legitimacy made it difficult for him to govern and the tensions and uprisings seen prior to the US invasion remained a fixture of Panamanian politics.

The first firm step toward democracy occurred during the 1994 presidential elections which were the first completely free elections since 1968. (124) The winner of the 1994 election, Ernesto Pérez Balladares inherited a number of problems.

> Panama has massive problems in education, housing and infrastructure and has experienced sharp increases in crime and drug abuse. It has a heavy debt burden, is behind many Latin American nations in the privatization process and is not part of any regional trading bloc. The Constitution needs major revisions and the government operates through a bloated bureaucracy, staffed through political favoritism and lacking any solid base of professional civil servants. (Millett 1994, 21)

Although Pérez Balladares was a Torrijos protégé, he did not completely follow his mentor's socialist policies and implemented an array of free-market reforms. Despite not completely mirroring Torrijos' policies, his major political problem was that since Panama has a multiparty system and he ran as part of a coalition, he only received about one-third of the popular meaning for many the legitimacy problems of Endara continued. Secondly, Pérez Balladares was a member of the PRD (Revolutionary Democratic Party) which was, in essence, the party of the previous dictatorships.

> At the heart of the dilemmas facing post-election Panama is the history of the PRD. Created by General Omar Torrijos as the political vehicle for his own peculiar version of military reformism, the party became, in the 1980s, the political arm for the dictatorship of General Manuel Antonio Noriega. It was bitterly hated by Panama's traditional ruling elites, and was perceived by Washington as a dangerous conglomerate of crooks and leftists. Many of its leaders were imprisoned or fled into exile following the 1989 US invasion which ended Noriega's rule, and the party's remnants were discredited, divided and seemingly doomed to political extinction. (21)

These problems were too much for Pérez Balladares to overcome and his presidency ended as so many do, in Panama and elsewhere, in a shambles, despite achieving economic growth of 4 percent a year during his tenure. (Harding 2006, 128)

In 1999 Panama made history when it elected the first female president in its history, Mireya Moscoso, the widow of Arnulfo Arias. The election of Moscoso signaled a move toward the populist policies favored by the Arnulfistas and a move away from the neoliberalism of Pérez Balladares. (130) It was also under the Moscoso Administration that the canal was turned over to Panama, which was not only an expansive responsibility, but also came with a range of security concerns. These included protecting the canal as well as issues of drug trafficking which had not gotten much better since the fall of Noriega, particularly with respect to corruption as "her administration was one of the most corrupt the country has ever had." (Velázquez 2006, 50) In addition, the problems related to the canal and security were so dire that, despite the near constant tensions between the United States and Panama over a variety of matters, the Moscoso Administration tried to convince the Americans to leave a military force, but the United States declined. (Harding 2006, 130)

THE LEGACIES OF PANAMANIAN HISTORY

The history of Panama is unique to the region and while it shares some similarities with its neighbors in Central America, it is different in many important ways. The most important difference between Panama and its neighbors is Panama's specific geographical location and the way that has affected its history and politics. The possibility of a canal and then the canal itself has dominated Panama since the Spaniards dreamed of an easier way to transport New World gold back to Spain. When the United States was finally able to accomplish the gargantuan task of building the canal, it left an indelible mark on Panama. The dynamics of US-Panamanian relations is the key to understanding the historic development of Panama

> because Panamanian historical consciousness has been shaped by a sustained critical engagement with US politics and interventions, as these have affected local political life in previous periods. In this respect, and in terms of the wider process of ethnic identity construction that took place during the twentieth century, the United States has been, from the point of view of Panamanians, Panama's most significant Other. (Theodossopoulos 2010, 55)

In fact, US involvement left such a strong mark that "many in Panama agree that there has been a tendency in practically all sectors of Panamanian society to assume that the United States would solve any problem in Panama." (Harding 2006, 136) This attitude is very interesting given that one of the most important threads running through US-Panamanian relations has been a lot of tension between the two countries, much of which is barely, if at all, "under the surface." Exemplifying the complicated nature of US-Panamanian relations is the fact that many Panamanians were quite glad to be rid of Noriega, but upset that it was done by the same foreign power that had dominated Panama for a century. Despite these tensions, the United States and Panama work closely in a number of areas including counternarcotics operations; extensive US foreign aid to assist Panama in social, economic, and political development; and a free trade agreement (FTA) that entered into force in 2012. (Sullivan 2012)

Another way that the United States and the construction of the canal left a lasting legacy in Panama is the diversity of the Panamanian population which includes in addition to the mestizo majority, West Indians, whites, and a sizeable indigenous population. In addition, intervention by the United States meant that ethnic conflict in Panama coalesced around national origin and thus Panamanian society has not suffered from high levels of ethnic conflict between its indigenous and mestizo populations like in other countries in Central America with a high population of indigenous people. Wickstrom (2003) argues that "while the Guatemalan state, for example, has formulated various attempts to exterminate indigenous communities over the decades, Panama has mostly attempted to encapsulate and assimilate them." (32)

The turnover of the canal to Panama in 1999 was an opportunity for US-Panamanian relations to begin anew as "the return of the canal has provided Panamanians with the prospect of forgiving US colonial transgressions that occurred in the past and investing constructively in their relationships with individual American citizens in the present." (Theodossopoulos 2010, 55) In addition, the most important legacy of US involvement in the canal itself, which Panama has managed since 1999. While providing much needed revenue to the government, the cost of maintenance and the expansion project begun in July of 2009 at a cost of US$5.2 billion (Schexnader 2014, 1) are daunting.

The upgrade is necessary because the canal was designed to accommodate ships that can carry 5,000 standard shipping containers while the Suez Canal can accommodate ships with 13,000 and today there are ships that carry as many as 18,000. (The Economist 2014, 29) In addition, modern oil tankers are approximately five times larger than the canal can accommodate, rendering it of little value to the oil industry (Kilian 2014) and creating a large competitive disadvantage for the Panama Canal. In addition, there are is also talk of reviving the idea of a second canal across Central America through Nicaragua. The Nicaraguan Canal is a joint project between a Chinese-owned firm and the Nicaraguan government which was slated to begin in December of 2014 at an estimated cost of US$60 billion. (Guillot 2014, 7) If this second Central American canal were to come to fruition, it would provide yet another competitor to Panama. Another of the negative legacies of the canal is its high environmental impact. "Upon leaving Panama, the US military left behind over 17,000 contaminated sites containing unexploded munitions throughout the canal. One test area alone—West Balboa Range—contained more than 50,000 pieces of contaminated ordinance." (Harding 2006, 131)

One of the most important legacies of Panamanian history is its openness to the outside world. Starting early in its independence, Panama sought ways to work with the outside world and to find ways to attract outside investment. This legacy of foreign investment as exemplified by the construction of the canal manifests itself today in the outward-looking nature of the Panamanian economy. Since the canal has dominated Panamanian history and economy it also stunted the growth of the economy in other areas, among them tourism. Due to the canal, most people thought of Panama as a transit point rather than a place to linger. This legacy is exemplified by the fact that a cruise through the canal is Panama's most popular tourist attraction.

THE PANAMANIAN ECONOMY

> The World Bank characterizes Panama as a middle income country with a GDP (PPP) per capita of $20,892 with recent growth rates of just above 6% for 2014 and 2015. These rates of growth are among the highest in the region and averaged 7.2% a year from 2001–2013. This level of economic growth allowed Panama to reduce the poverty rate from 39.9% in 2007 to 26.2% in 2012. A lot of Panama's success has been due to its open economy and its ability to attract foreign direct investment and, most especially, to their success in running the canal which is the centerpiece of their economy. (US Department of State 2015, 3)

Since Panama's geography has always dominated its place in the world, the Panamanian economy has long been dependent on the rest of the world utilizing its territory as a transit point for their own shipping. Starting in the colonial period when the region served as the shipment point for gold and silver from Peru to Spain to the centrality of the Panama Canal to the its economy today, Panama has long been dependent on world commerce. Panama's unique attributes meant that they did not develop the sort of agriculture based economies of its neighbors until much later in its history. This reliance has made the Panamanian economy particularly prone to downturns in the world economy and the cyclical nature of trade. These broad, cyclical trends include Panama's economic decline in the 1700s as colonial exchange diminished with the depletion of New World gold and silver mines then increased in the mid-eighteenth century as the California gold rush increased the amount of supplies sent across the isthmus as people pursued their fortunes on the west coast of the United States.

Since its completion in 1914, the canal has dominated Panama's economy both when it was run by the United States and since Panama took over operations in December 1999. The completion of the canal greatly increased inter-coastal trade for the United States and for much of South America, which used the canal due to the rugged nature of their interiors. In 1914 and 1915 there were approximately 5.5 million tons of shipping through the canal. By 1924 shipping had increased to 23 million tons and peaked at 31 million in 1929 before falling with the onset of the Great Depression in 1930. In the depths of the Great Depression in 1932, shipping fell to 18 million tons through the canal but had essentially returned to normal by 1935 and 1936. (Mason and Rowlands 1938, 326–27) While US shipping through the canal was down slightly, the majority of the downturn was due to countries other than the United States whose economies had essentially ground to a standstill. It is estimated that the Great Depression caused a 40 percent decline in business through the canal for the first half of the 1930s. (Manfredo 1993, 103)

Due to this, and similarly to other small economies, particularly in Latin America, the Great Depression hit Panama especially hard. Due to the relationship between the United States and Panama with respect to the canal, the Great Depression also caused a lot of tension between the two countries. "Unemployment was widespread and, in May (1933) President Harmodio Arias announced the suspension of interest payments on one of two of Panama's two main American debts." (Major 1985, 358) Throughout the 1930s, Panama's grievances regarding revenues gleaned from the canal continued to affect US-Panamanian relations, however by the end of the decade, the United States' concerns began to center on the security of the canal with the outbreak of World War II in Europe and Asia.

While still unhappy in their economic relationship with the United States with respect to the canal, World War II gave the Panamanian economy a boost via increased US spending in the Canal Zone to ensure that the canal would not fall into enemy hands. A number of measures adopted by the Franklin Delano Roosevelt Administration in 1939 and 1940 boosted the US presence in the canal despite its ostensible neutrality. These measures included, an increase in US forces, negotiations with neighboring states in the case of aggression against the canal including the existence of airplane facilities near the canal, the establishment of naval patrols and the mining of some canal terminals. There were also a number of measures that limited the movements of certain nationalities through the canal. (Padelford 1941, 88)

After a brief economic downturn when US soldiers defending the canal departed, Panama experienced a post–World War II boom as the world economy expanded from the 1950s to the 1970s and the expansion of the world economy was a boon for the canal. With the "tremendous growth in the US economy, the 'economic miracle of Japan,' and the spurring development and growth in many other economies as well, the Panama Canal found itself playing a critical role in postwar recovery." (Manfredo 1993, 103) The increased revenue through the canal helped to stimulate other parts of the Panamanian economy such as agriculture, manufacturing, and tourism. With this rapid postwar economic expansion, the Panamanian grew an average of 6.4 percent a year between 1950 and 1970. (Tollefson 1989, 127)

The 1970s illustrated some of the weaknesses of Panama's economy and reliance on external actors as annual GDP growth began to fall due to "reduced canal use, rising oil prices, international inflation, and recession in the major industrial countries." (130) In addition, the Torrijos government had spent large sums of money on health and education policies financed in large part by foreign loans. "Panama had taken out 12 successive loans from the International Monetary Fund and had accumulated over $1 billion in debt, reaching 12 percent of GDP." (Harding 2006, 86) A familiar story throughout Latin America, Panama's spending in the decades after World War II financed by international loans, meant that the 1980s would be a "lost decade" for Panama, one in which persistent economic problems would erode many of the social, political, and economic gains of the previous decades. For Panama, things were worse still with the regime of Manuel Noriega who ruled the economy as his own neopatrimonial empire, or as an Israeli intelligence officer quipped about Noriega "Panama is a funny country . . . it's not really a country. It's more like a business . . . I know the storekeeper." (94)

The aftermath of the 1980s was even more difficult for the Panamanian economy due to the deterioration of US-Panamanian relations and the destruction wrought by the US invasion to remove Noriega in 1989. "After years of economic sanctions as well as the destruction and looting following the US invasion, the amount of economic aid needed to rebuild Panama's tattered economy was estimated at more than $2 billion." (120) In addition, the government of Panama was fully aware that running the canal would be a monumental task and that the United States had provided a sizable amount of money to Panama's economy as well as thousands of jobs. "Prior to the 1990s the US military personnel's spending in Panama contributed around 5 percent of Panama's GDP, and around 75,000 Panamanians depended on income from the bases and businesses serving the bases." (121) While the Panama Canal represents a major economic asset for Panama as well as a vital world trade link, it is not immune from events in world markets that make shipping more dangerous or costly such as economic downturns, war and changes in the cost of oil.

Another major legacy of US involvement with the canal is that the Panamanian economy has used the US dollar as its currency since 1904 when the US dollar and the Panamanian Balboa were fixed at a 1:1 ratio, with the dollar as the medium of exchange and the Balboa as a unit of account. (Moreno-Villalaz 1999, 421) Scholars are fairly well united in the idea that Panama has benefitted significantly from dollarizing their economy from an economic standpoint, however politically dollarization not only abdicates monetary policy to a foreign country but also means that if US-Panamanian relations suffer it can cause an array of economic problems. For instance, Cohen (2003) argues that

> in economic terms, most observers have rightly had only praise for Panama's currency dependence. Reliance on the dollar has created an environment of

> stability that has both suppressed inflation—a bane of most of Panama's hemispheric neighbors—and helped establish the country as an important offshore financial center. But in political terms Panama has been extremely vulnerable in its relations with Washington, which of course could sour at any moment. (230)

Given the frequent tensions in US-Panamanian relations, political problems between the two nations can quickly spill over into economic problems for Panama. The most acute example of this occurred as the United States began to apply pressure to the Noriega regime and ultimately depose him. Relations between the United States and Noriega hit a breaking point in 1988 and 1989 when "the United States imposed trade sanctions, stopped passing along revenue from the Panama Canal, froze Panamanian bank deposits in the United States and ceased shipping US currency to Panama. Panama's economy suffered a severe recession, and a shortage of currency occurred." (Schuler 2003, 145)

The dollarization of the Panamanian economy for such a long time has created a very unique situation in which Panama "[embodies], as no other country, freedom of choice in the capital markets." (Moreno-Villalaz 2005, 127) The freedom of choice and general openness has helped Panama achieve a growth rate that outpaces its neighbors. "With average annual growth rates of 8.5 percent, Panama's per capita GDP has more than doubled over the past decade." (International Monetary Fund 2015) This growth is facilitated by a general sense of fiscal discipline among recent Panamanian presidents, and also due to the financial discipline created by dollarization in which Panamanian politicians do not have the option of printing currency to solve budgetary problems because without a central banking system, this is impossible. Another reason that the dollarized exchange rate has been a success for Panama is that they are not a large producer of goods, but instead serves as an intermediary focused on services. Due to this "a revaluation or devaluation of the dollar tends to shift demand from imported US goods to imported Japanese goods (or vice versa)—without affecting the real effective exchange rate." (Moreno-Villalaz 2005, 127)

With such a large amount of economic activity centered on services and with the Panama Canal drawing a good deal of Panama's FDI, the Canal and its operation has tended to push other industries and entrepreneurship to the periphery of the Panamanian economy. "Panama does not appear to emphasize or realize entrepreneurship with an equal intensity. This may be because Panama has its Canal to manage and prioritize. The Canal has proved to be very lucrative for Panama, and with this asset Panama may not feel compelled to plan for long-term growth through entrepreneurship, but through the Canal itself." (Thurston, Hackney, and Boggs 2013, 72) This lack of entrepreneurship in Panama as a result of the canal has had a profound negative effect on manufacturing. Due to the country's historic evolution, which focused resources overwhelmingly on services and transactions, the assembly and manufacturing sectors—largely comprised of production of items such as processed foods, chemical products, construction materials, and a small and declining clothing sector—remain severely underdeveloped. Panamanian export industries across the board make up a surprisingly small amount of the export economy. Looking at the sector data, as a result of the canal, in addition to the service sector at 78.4 percent of GDP, this is followed by industry at 17.9 percent, and most surprisingly agriculture at a miniscule 3.7 percent. (US Commercial Service 2013)

One of the most surprising aspects of the Panamanian economy is the minimal impact of agriculture on the overall economy, which is quite different from its neighbor's very strong reliance on agro-export. Despite its small contribution to GDP, agriculture does provide 17 percent of the total jobs in the Panamanian economy and is more important in rural areas where it supports about 40 percent of the rural population. (Field 2007, 14–15) This means that while agriculture does not contribute a large percentage to the Panamanian economy, it does provide jobs in rural areas in which poverty is already quite high. Not surprisingly while a small part of the economy, the Panamanian agricultural sector is protected by government policy and is uncompetitive on the international market. (Hornbeck 2012, 8)

Despite an open economy and extensive foreign direct investment, there are aspects of starting a business in Panama that can be very difficult and the government of Panama should take measures to make it easier for people to start businesses as many aspects of starting a running a business in Panama do not rate high versus the rest of the world.

These ratings reflect that while Panama is an open economy with a somewhat conducive business climate, there is a large amount of government corruption and inefficiency. In addition, these rankings also reflect the fact that while it is relatively easy to start a business as reflected in the raking for credit, utilities, and some licensing, it is much more difficult to run the business once it is open due to issues with the enforcement of the rule of law and the difficulties in the taxes system. This combination of economic openness and government inefficiency and corruption is something that urgently needs to be remedied.

THE DEVELOPMENT OF ECOTOURISM IN PANAMA

Although traditionally small, particularly outside of the Canal Zone and the Colón Free Zone, Panama's tourism industry has been growing over the last couple decades and now represents 5.9 percent of Panamanian GDP and is predicted to almost double by 2024. (World Trade and Travel Council 2014,

Table 4.1. Doing Business in Panama

Topics	*DB 2016 Rank*	*DB 2015 Rank*
Starting a Business	44	37
Dealing with Construction Permits	70	67
Getting Electricity	32	31
Registering Property	84	81
Getting Credit	19	17
Protecting Minority Investors	66	64
Paying Taxes	166	166
Trading Across Borders	54	53
Enforcing Contracts	148	147
Resolving Insolvency	132	131

Source: World Bank Doing Business Rankings, rank out of 189.

3) Panamanian tourism mainly caters to two sets of tourists, those who visit Panama for a fixed amount of time and those who visit Panama while in transit through the canal. Panama is blessed with a variety of possibilities for visitors interested in ecotourism and cultural tourism. In an article published in *The Geographical Journal* in 1973 anticipating the building of Pan-American Highway, P. J. K. Burton notes the potential of ecotourism in Panama:

> Positive action could also be taken by fostering the tourist attractions of the area and its wildlife. This may never equal the spectacle of the African plains with their herds of large mammals; nevertheless, there is a considerable potential. Few people get the opportunity to experience the fascination of a tropical forest at first hand, and the jungles of Darien, rendered accessible by road, could admirably fill this need. Such tourism need not be restricted to the dry season. Americans and Europeans living in Panama with whom we have spoken unanimously consider the wet seasons the most pleasant time of year. Accommodation of a high standard would, of course, be necessary, but this should not prove an insuperable difficulty. Special observation facilities such as tree-top observation towers would be an added attraction. (50)

The first government attempt to establish a tourist trade in Panama came in 1934 via Law 79 which created the National Tourism Commission made up entirely of representatives from the private sector charged with helping to organize and promote the arrival of a large number of foreigners into Panama. This arrangement was later modified to include relevant government bodies such as the Secretary of Labor, Trade, and Industry and the Panama City Council. (Gobierno Nacional, Republica de Panama) Unlike many countries whose early attempts to build a tourist industry focused on visiting researchers and a small number of foreign tourists, the presence of the canal meant that there was a steady flow of a relatively large number of foreign visitors passing through the country.

Despite these early attempts at organizing tourism in Panama, there was still only marginal foreign interest in doing anything other than passing through the canal. In fact the National Tourism Commission was created and then quickly disbanded due to budgetary issues. In 1960 the government of Panama passed Law 22 creating the Panamanian Tourism Institute (IPAT) to boost the tourism industry. This second attempt at a national tourism agency was much more successful as this new organization was given a much wider set of powers and a much greater amount of autonomy in promoting tourism. (Gobierno Nacional, Republica de Panama) To this day, IPAT is the primary government agency that deals with promoting Panamanian tourism.In its role as the chief promoter of tourism IPAT has the following functions:

1. Encourage, coordinate, facilitate, participate, promote, monitor, protect, and establish everything related to tourism.
2. Facilitate the entrance and a pleasant stay in Panama for foreign visitors seeking relaxation, amusement, and entertainment
3. Encourage domestic tourism among residents of the Republic.
4. Promote the construction and maintenance of places of recreation for use by tourists.
5. Produce information necessary to publicize the country in order to attract tourism.
6. Regulate tourist activities to protect the interests of tourists while in Panama. (Gobierno Nacional, Republica de Panama)

The most important attraction for the use of sustainable ecotourism as a development strategy is the use of the Panama Canal as an ecotourism destination, trips through the canal are gaining in popularity and an internet search nets myriad options for tourists who desire to take a cruise through the canal via US ports with the most common starting in Florida and ending in California. The problem with using the canal as a destination for ecotourists is that its environmental impact limits the ability of the canal to contribute to sustainable ecotourism.

Heckadon Moreno (1993) states that the biggest environmental problems in and around the Canal—specifically in the Chagres River Basin—are population growth, mining, industrialization, urbanization, and road construction. (132) While important problems on their own, each also exacerbates problems of deforestation in and around the Chagres River Basin and Gatun Lake which serves as a reservoir for water used in the canal. Another important issue is the use of water by the Panama Canal Authority as approximately 52 million gallons are released into the Atlantic and Pacific oceans with each of the thirty-five to forty-five ships that transit the Canal each day. (Carse 2012, 539) This water is drawn for rainfall in the surrounding area, however deforestation has lowered the amount of water collected making it necessary to store larger amounts so the canal can function. Given the impact of the Canal on the environment, particularly after the planned expansion, the government of Panama's ability to limit the these negative impacts will be a key determinant of whether or not Panama will be able to develop sustainable ecotourism related to the canal.

Panama has a lot of potential both from its indigenous groups as well as from its long history as a major hemispheric trading location to develop as a cultural and historical tourism destination. One of the best examples of this potential is the *Camino Real* which served as a major thoroughfare during colonialism and is located in an area with a rich history from pre-Columbian cultures to the time of the Conquistadores complete with a history of mule trains and pirate attacks and therefore provides the ideal raw material for the creation of a cultural tourism destination. (Strassnig 2010, 166) In addition, Panama could develop a cultural tourism industry similar to the *Ruta Maya* in southern Mexico, Belize, and Guatemala.

As evident in Table 4.2, tourism in Panama has grown significantly over the course of the twenty-first century. What is particularly impressive is that the growth in tourist arrivals do not appear to have been affected by the 2008–2009 global recession.

One of the most attractive parts of developing an ecotourism industry in Panama is that the tourism sector has the highest multiplier effect on the economy—nearly double that of Colón and the Canal—because of very high backward and forward linkages. The sector also has a large potential to benefit the poor; most of the gains in household incomes from the Colón Free Zone, the Canal, and other sectors of the economy accrue to urban nonpoor households while the poor earn a far greater share of the total increase in incomes from tourism. (Klytchnikova and Dorosh 2013, 78) In spite of the expanding number of tourists visiting Panama, the government has decided to focus on luxury tourism rather than something that more closely resembles sustainable ecotourism. This policy was made clear in the Strategic Plan 2010–2014, which advocated a focus on destinations with a higher potential to become world-class and luxury destinations. In order to accomplish this, Panama will focus on the south coast of Farallon, the Perlas Islands, and Panama City. (Government of Panama 2015, 62)

With the development of Panamanian economy strongly centered on the Panama Canal and manner in which tourism in Panama grew over time, they do not appear to be well equipped to develop into a sustainable ecotourism destination. With most of the focus on visitors who pass through the Canal and traditionally very few overnight tourists, Panama has a lot of work to do

Table 4.2. Tourist Arrivals to Panama

Year	Total Visitors
2003	566,000
2004	621,000
2005	702,000
2006	843,000
2007	1,103,000
2008	1,247,000
2009	1,200,000
2010	1,324,000
2011	1,473,000
2012	1,606,000
2013	1,658,000

Source: World Bank 2015.

to grow beyond the Canal and the Colón Free Zone. In some ways, given Panama's unique history they have skipped over an intermediate level of development in which small-scale tourism businesses proliferate and have gone from early tourism development centered on cruise passengers to high-end luxury tourism. This trajectory is different from Costa Rica and Belize which developed small-scale tourism in which local ownership proliferated prior to moving on to incorporate other forms of tourism. The government of Panama's Strategic Plan for 2015–2019 barely mentions tourism policies and simply focuses on ways to advance the sector by improvements in marketing, training of tourism employees, and infrastructure. (Government of Panama 2015)

FOREIGN DIRECT INVESTMENT IN PANAMA

Given its status as a transit point for shipping throughout virtually all of its history, Panama is uniquely integrated into the world economy and in many ways the Panama Canal represents one of the largest foreign investments in history. As such, throughout most of its history Panama has been a popular destination for foreign direct investment and has aggressively sought out investors for a variety of projects. (US Department of State 2015, 3)

The government agency charged with attracting investment to Panama is the *Agencia de Promoción de Inversiones y Exportaciones* (PROINVEX). It was created to simplify the process for firms that want to invest in virtually any sector of the Panamanian economy with an emphasis on sectors identified as engines of economic growth in the government of Panama's "Strategic Plan of Government." (PROINVEX) These "engines of economic growth" identified in the Strategic Plan of Government 2015–2019 are logistics and transport, agriculture and tourism. (Government of Panama 2014, 3)

One of the ways in which the government is able to attract foreign investment to Panama is through policies of nondiscrimination such as the Investment Stability Act which was passed as Law 54 on July 22, 1998. This law explicitly states that foreign investment is not treated any differently from domestic investment and that they have the same rights and obligations as national investors and companies including commerce and industry freedom as well as the ability to import and export. (PROINVEX) In addition, PROINVEX issues an Industrial Promotion Certificate to attract companies to Panama for research and development, environmental management programs, investment in utilities, training in human resources, and employment. The benefits of this program include a 35 percent reduction in taxes for agricultural-industrial companies and 25 percent for all other industrial activities. In addition, this program provides a preferential 3 percent tariff for the importation of capital goods. PROINVEX also prioritizes the development of offshore call centers as well as incentives to encourage film companies to make movies in Panama. (PROINVEX)

In addition, Panama offers a variety of incentives and tax benefits for companies that locate there.

> Official support for investment and business activity is especially strong for the Colón Free Zone (CFZ), the banking sector, the tourism sector, and the free zones. Companies in the CFZ pay basic user fees and a 5 percent dividend tax (or 2 percent of net profits if there are no dividends). Banks and individuals in Panama pay no tax on interest or other income earned outside Panama. No taxes are withheld on savings or fixed time deposits in Panama. Individual depositors do not pay taxes on time deposits. Free zones offer tax-free status, special immigration privileges, and license and customs exemptions to manufacturers who locate there. Investment incentives offered by the GOP are available equally to Panamanian and foreign investors. The incentives do not discriminate or distinguish between Panamanians and foreign investors. (US Department of State 2015, 18)

As the numbers illustrate, Panama has been able to attract an increasing amount of foreign direct investment since they took over operation of the Canal.

Table 4.3. Foreign Direct Investment to Panama

Year	FDI by Year in USD Millions
2000	623.9
2001	467.1
2002	98.6
2003	81.7
2004	1,019
2005	1,104
2006	2,936
2007	2,023
2008	2,454
2009	1,085
2010	2,549
2011	4,395
2012	3,297
2013	5,053
2014	5,213

Source: World Bank 2015.

Within the history of relations between the United States and Panama, the United States is the largest foreign investor in the Panamanian economy and their economic relationship became closer when the two countries signed a free-trade agreement (FTA) in 2007 that came into force in 2012. The United States–Panama Trade Promotion Agreement is a comprehensive and reciprocal trade agreement that replaced a number of other free-trade treaties between the two countries and has led to a much more liberalized economy. In addition, Panama has also pursued FTAs with Mexico and the European Union and has been able to an reach an agreement with Colombia. Panama is also pursuing membership in the Pacific Alliance. This protrade posture has further increased Panama's openness to foreign investment and has provided new protections and privileges for foreign investors. (US Department of State 2015, 3)

Under the US-Panama FTA 88 percent of US commercial and industrial exports will be duty free with tariffs on the other products phased out over a ten-year period. In addition over 50 percent of US farm exports will be immediately duty free. The FTA also covers telecommunications, trade in services, government procurement, investment, and intellectual property. (Hornbeck 2012, NP) Panama was interested in signing an FTA with the United States despite a relatively small industrial export sector because "like other countries pursuing an FTA with the United States, Panama seeks closer ties for the continued FDI that may be generated from having a permanent rules-based trade relationship with a large trading partner." (12) This is due in large part to the fact that 78.4 percent of Panamanian GDP (US Commercial Service 2013) is derived from the service sector and the infrastructure necessary for the Canal requires a great deal of outside investment. This is also why Panama wanted to have a stand-alone agreement rather than be attached to an FTA with the United States and other countries.

The US-Panama FTA joins with the Colón Free Zone (CFZ), which after Hong Kong is the largest duty free zone in the world. (10) Situated on the Atlantic side of the canal, the CFV is used as a re-exportation center for much of the rest of the world. Its economic impact on Panama is significant as it contains over 2,500 companies operating within its 450 hectares and is serviced by five local ports as well as the Inter-American highway. Each year the CFZ handles more than US$16 billion in imports and re-exports each year and employs more than 28,000 people. (Colón Free Zone)

Over its history, Panama has been uniquely integrated into the international economy and as such has developed a highly open economy in an attempt to attract foreign direct investment in a variety of sectors. While the development of tourism in Panama over its history has made more environmentally conscious forms of tourism less likely, the success of the Panamanian economy in attracting outside investment means that these numbers will likely only go up. Due to this, Panama is poised to emerge as a regional leader in a variety of services, most especially shipping and finance.

FACTORS THAT ENCOURAGE ECOTOURISM DEVELOPMENT AND FOREIGN DIRECT INVESTMENT

Over its history, the economic policies of Panama have focused almost completely on the administration of the canal to the exclusion of many other economic pursuits. Despite this, the number of tourists traveling to Panama is growing and it has many of the features needed to attract ecotourists. Due to Panama's long relationship with the United States and its ability to attract foreign direct investment, many of the basic parts are in place for Panama to cultivate sustainable ecotourism, however tourism development is at a crossroads. Panama has a much longer history of attracting foreign investment and is well known to investors as a safe foreign location for their money. One of the primary factors that facilitate foreign investment is the stability of the government of Panama.

Despite the fact that for much of its history, democracy has been a "work in progress" for Panama the country has made great strides in consolidating democracy. In particular, since the removal of Manuel Noriega by US forces in 1989, there has been a marked improvement in the democratic stability and the rule of law. Both of these factors are fundamental to attracting eco-tourists and investors. In addition, while Panama has an open economy and many positive attributes, it also has many areas that need work.

> Panama is plagued by a poor educational system, high labor costs, a lack of skilled workers, and consistent reports of corruption, fraud, and a lack of judicial transparency. Foreign investors in Panama have complained about a lack of transparency in the government procurement process and struggle to resolve investment disputes through the courts. Because so many investors have had trouble with Panama's court system, most lawyers recommend including binding arbitration clauses in contracts. US firms have reported inconsistent, unfair, and biased treatment from Panamanian courts which continue to be subject to corruption. (US Department of State 2015, 3)

For the most part, the problem with the rule of law in Panama is more concerning to investors than to tourists and although private property rights are deeply ensconced in Panamanian law sometimes they are not fully realized. This is due in large part to a high level of corruption throughout every level of government, with Transparency International giving Panama a score of 37 out of 100 in its 2014 Corruption Perceptions Index. (Transparency International 2015) Particularly troubling is corruption in the judicial branch which often manifests itself as "impunity for clients linked to the main political parties, former officials and other people of influence." (Justiniani 2007, 252) In addition, despite an array of anticorruption laws on the books, very few people are ever charged with a crime and fewer still are prosecuted. Due to this "the general perception is that anti-corruption laws are not applied rigorously, and that government enforcement bodies and the courts are not effective in pursuing and prosecuting those accused of corruption, particularly in high profile cases." (US Department of State 2015, 16)

Corruption in Panama is exacerbated by the openness of the Panamanian economy, which has made Panama a major source of money laundering and even put it on the "gray list" of countries that have deficiencies in anti–money laundering laws as well as financing for terrorism by the Financial Action Task Force (FATF). In June 2014, Panama made an action plan to take measures to end widespread money laundering in its banking system, which seeks to be a banking hub for the region. These include criminalizing all forms of money laundering and establishing a legal framework for freezing assets of offenders, measures to improve transparency, a fully functional financial intelligence unit, and mechanisms to better discover suspicious transactions. (Financial Action Task Force) It is important that Panama adequately address these issues in order to improve the climate of the rule of law and to tighten their banking laws so investors have a greater amount of faith in the system.

Problems of money laundering are also a legacy of the Noriega years in which Panama was a major transit point for drugs coming into the United States, a problem that persists to this day. "Panama's strategic geographic location, dollarized economy, status as a regional financial, trade, and logistics center; and lax regulatory system make it an attractive target for money launderers. Money laundering in Panama is believed to come in part from the proceeds of drug trafficking due to the country's location along major drug trafficking routes." (US Department of State 2015, 7) Government attempts to alleviate the drug trade have been ongoing since the end of the Noriega regime and have shown some signs of success. *The FBI Law Enforcement Bulletin* calls the cooperation between Panama and US officials "a model of success in the drug war" because "operation Panama Express has resulted in the seizure of over 500 tons of cocaine worth an estimated $10 billion [USD]. Authorities have arrested more than 2,000 international drug traffickers and transporters, mostly Colombians. Additionally, pending capture at open sea, transporters have dropped to the bottom of the Pacific Ocean another 391 tons of cocaine worth another $7 billion [USD]." (Thomas 2011, 1)

Despite these problems, the United States Department of State Bureau of Diplomatic Security states that "Panama remains relatively safe when compared to other Latin American countries, although crime rates are higher than one would encounter in much of the US." (United States Department of State Bureau of Diplomatic Security 2015) In particular, Panama has been able to improve its police force and has begun to shed the image it acquired during the Noriega years. A great deal of the improvement in Panama's security apparatus, including its police, stems from reforms made after the US invasion to ensure that various security actors would be depoliticized. The changes to the Panamanian security forces after Noriega was removed from office were equal parts a "demilitarization" process, a police reform and a transition to democracy. (Caumartin 2007, 107)

Another area in need of reform is the Panamanian educational system, which has been plagued by a variety of problems since Panama became independent from Colombia. This first educational system would both reflect as well as reinforce many of the class-based biases that still affect Panama to this day as the school system was segregated by social class. (Harris 2007, 16) This system would also serve to further isolate Panama's rural population, including a large number of indigenous peoples, from Panamanians who resided in the city. Under pressure from the United States, in 1920 the class-based system was replaced by a more inclusive system. (16)

The United States had a vested interest in the Panamanian educational system as a large number of Panamanians worked on the Canal, whose operation was of the utmost importance to the United States. Similarly, as Panama turns its attention to a globalized economy based on the development of sustainable ecotourism and foreign direct investment, it is necessary for the Panamanian educational system to prepare its workers for the twenty-first century. Currently, Panama has a 95 percent literacy rate among adults fifteen years and older, with virtually equal rates between men and women. (CIA World Factbook) Despite the high literacy rate, the Panamanian educational system is rife with problems. According to the US Department of State:

> Despite spending of approximately 12.6 percent of the central government budget and 2.5 percent of GDP on education, approximately half of students fail their university entrance exam. The 2013 World Economic Forum Global Competitiveness Report ranked Panama 68 out of 144 countries for quality of education and pointed to an inadequately educated workforce as the most problematic factor for doing business. This poor showing underscored the 2010 OECD Program for International Student Achievement (PISA) analysis, which ranked Panama second worst among participating Latin American countries. (US Department of State 2015, 18)

As a result of the problems in education, it is often difficult for companies in Panama find the workers they need to operate a business. Without an educated and productive workforce, Panama will find it increasingly difficult to attract foreign investment as well as find people to work in sustainable ecotourism. One of the reasons that Costa Rica has been able to successfully grow its ecotourism industry over the last two decades is that their educational system focuses on skills that will aid workers in the tourism industry such as English language, technical skills, and environmental education. The lack of an educated labor force also forces businesses in Panama to invite foreign workers when the domestic labor market cannot provide an adequate workforce. Acknowledging this problem, Panamanian banking executive Raul Aleman stated "the lack of skilled labor obligates businesses to bring in foreign labor, which is more costly for them and of little benefit for our country." (Mattson and Teran, 2015)

Since the government of Panama already spends a good deal of the national budget on education, Panama is better able to focus on the problem areas without the need to allocate more funds. Among the biggest issues that need to be addressed are access to education, particularly among the country's poor and indigenous populations and instructional effectiveness. In 2006 the Inter-American Development Bank initiated the Education Development Project (PRODE) to improve education in Panama.

> The objective of the reformulated IDB project is to improve both educational opportunities and learning conditions for all, but especially for those from disadvantaged backgrounds. This is to be achieved through the creation of new educational opportunities for these groups, through increased quality and inclusiveness of education and through the establishment of adequate learning facilities, as well as through a secondary education reform. (Harris 2007, 21)

In addition the Inter-American Development Bank project also seeks to improve the skills of the Panamanian workforce in areas directly related to their economy. For instance, reforms at the high school level will add curriculum in an industrial concentration, telecommunications and maritime ports and transportation. (20) The success of this program have been mixed because: PRODE's implementation was continuously troubled by the complexity of its design, the low level of installed technical capacity in (Panama's Ministry of Education) and frequent rotations of staff in the executing unit, and cost overruns, which frustrated many of the efforts to improve execution and limited the expected results. (30) For Panama to fully embrace a global economy it is necessary for them to formulate a strategy that will help to fix the shortcomings in its educational system rather than continually spend money on it with very little results.

Since so much of the Panamanian economy is centered in transportation and related services, they have an infrastructure that is ranked among the best in Latin America ranking 45 out of 160 countries surveyed on the Logistics Performance Index (LPI) given by the World Bank. Obviously, the biggest infrastructure project in Panamanian history is the expansion of the Canal which will help to better serve larger ships and will help to facilitate cruise ship travel through the canal. In addition, in just under five hours a tourist can fly from New York's JFK airport to Panama City. The close proximity to the large markets of United States and Canada gives Panama an excellent comparative advantage for tourists from North America. The expansion of the Panama Canal will also help it to compete with any future canal through Nicaragua. Although the prospects for a Nicaraguan Canal appear to be fairly remote, if it came to fruition, it would represent a major challenge to the Panamanian economy as its proposed size would be able to serve larger vessels than the Panama Canal.

Panama has worked diligently to attract foreign direct investment and has created one of the most open economies in Latin America. The dollarization of the Panamanian economy helps to ensure an investment environment with relatively low inflation and little risk of loss due to foreign exchange for US-based investors. In addition, at the microeconomic level, dollarization greatly simplifies transaction for both visiting ecotourists as well as for investors. In many ways the Panamanian economy is focused on the attraction of outside investment and has benefitted extensively from economic liberalization.

COMPARATIVE ADVANTAGES AND FUTURE PROSPECTS

Given the macroeconomic climate in Panama, the country will likely continue to experience growth in foreign direct investment, however growth in the tourism industry, particularly in sustainable ecotourism is far less certain.

The biggest set of comparative advantages for foreign direct investment into Panama is the combination of the openness of the economy, the relationship of the canal to international trade, and the stability of the Panamanian economy as a result of dollarization. These factors have made Panama one of the best performing economies in Latin America. In 2014 Latin America saw a 39 percent decrease in foreign direct investment and a region wide growth rate of only .8 percent. Despite these numbers, Panama was the only state among the top ten in Latin America whose foreign direct investment numbers were higher than the previous years. (*Financial Times* 2015)

The openness of the Panamanian economy gives the government a major comparative advantage over other states in Latin America whose economies are far less open to the world or in the case of Venezuela, and increasingly Argentine, openly hostile. Not only is Panama easily outcompeting Venezuela for outside investment, Venezuelans wary of the behavior of their own government are investing in Panama. These investors seek the same tax benefits as other investors, however they also get a lot more stable investment environment. (Culshaw 2013, 74)

Due to the long relationship between Panama and the United States, Panamanians are quite familiar with US culture and English is widely spoken. The role of the United States in Panama created a love/hate relationship for Panamanians toward US citizens and many Panamanians will use a variety of positive and negative terms to describe Americans. For instance while Theodossopoulos (2010) found that Panamanians descriptions of Americans "call attention to a 'human' dimension of North Americans, developed in interpersonal relations, and portray a 'generous' kind of people, 'capable of taking care of and protecting other human beings, animals, or the environment.' He also found that 'the most common fault that Panamanians attribute to US citizens is their frequently criticized arrogance.'" (58) In addition, unlike tourism is Nicaragua, Panama does not have a "bad reputation" among US tourists and did not experience a recent civil war that is still fresh in the minds of many US tourists.

The future of tourism in Panama rests on three main pillars: traditional ecotourism, the Canal, and cultural tourism. The way in which these three tourism areas can coexist and prosper will say a lot about the future of growth in the Panamanian tourism industry. As its most obvious attraction, the Panama Canal will likely draw tourists for years to come and is Panama's most important comparative advantage. The extent to which these attractions adhere to the tenets of sustainable ecotourism is yet to be seen.

Chapter Five

Conclusion: The Future of Ecotourism Development in Central America

This chapter examines the case study information provided in the previous chapters in order to discern strategies and policy recommendations for states to utilize ecotourism as a development strategy. Particularly important are ways in which globalization, open market neoliberalism, and sustainable ecotourism interact with each other to spur economic growth and the extent to which ecotourism policies also help to attract foreign direct investment. Given that the ecotourism industry tends to be labor intensive, it can serve as a real catalyst for states that have tried (and failed) at other types of economic development models. In addition, the example of Costa Rica illustrates the need for a well thought out plan to spread the benefits of ecotourism development across as many segments of society as possible via the development of small-scale ecotourism enterprises and the need to stick to that plan.

GLOBALIZATION, NEOLIBERALISM, AND SUSTAINABLE ECOTOURISM IN CENTRAL AMERICA

Each of the case studies in this book illustrates the importance of states engaging with globalization and instituting free market neoliberal reforms that open their economies to the outside world. The expansion of policies that encourage the development of sustainable ecotourism and the attraction of foreign direct investment are vitally important because of the need for economic development in places that have long suffered from high rates of poverty. The use of sustainable ecotourism as a development strategy is unique because of its ability to create jobs across a number of skill levels and strata of society while also preserving the natural environment. Given the labor intensity of tourism development, the poor stand to benefit considerably; for instance, Klytchnikova and Dorosh (2013) argue that "the poor earn a far greater share of the total increase in incomes from tourism." (78) One of the key transformations in Costa Rica over the second half of the twentieth century was the shift from an economy mostly based on agricultural exports to one in which a large portion of GDP comes from ecotourism and high-tech manufacturing.

The need for economic development is particularly acute in Nicaragua because they have suffered for their entire history from abject poverty, with very little possibility of any real improvement. With the end of their civil war more than two decades ago, and the Somoza dynasty a distant memory, Nicaragua may finally be able to emerge from the cycles of violence and outside intervention that have plagued them since the colonial era. In addition, with the advent of globalization, small economies such as Nicaragua are now better situated to take advantage of their natural assets and attract tourists as a reliable source of export income. Given the difficulties for countries like Nicaragua to acquire the level of capital required for economic development, embracing a globalization and opening its economy to the world can be a new beginning.

Nicaragua is a particularly interesting case because of the growing number of tourists who visit and the government's success in attracting foreign direct investment despite the anti-US, antiglobalization, and antineoliberalism rhetoric emanating from Managua. Despite this rhetoric, Nicaragua has made great progress since the civil war in creating a stable environment for tourists and investors by opening itself to the world—something that Nicaragua has significantly benefitted from. The key questions for Nicaragua's future is whether or not it can consolidate democracy and the rule of law and whether Sandinistas other than Daniel Ortega will work to undo the free market policies carried out by the Ortega Administration. As Ortega has increasingly distanced himself from some of the civil war era Sandinista leaders, it is difficult to predict what a Sandinista-controlled Nicaragua without Ortega would look like. Hopefully, given the progress Nicaragua has shown since the end of the civil war will give it the inertia to continue down the same path.

Belize is an interesting case study because as one of the smallest economies in the world, it has a unique set of problems, most significantly its small range of export products which makes it especially prone to external shocks. Since Belize's economy is the 167th largest economy in the world (out of 189) (World Bank 2015) it is highly dependent on the outside world and despite spending a lot of its history in isolation, Belize has embraced globalization and opened its economy to outside investment. As a very small economy, Belize must formulate policies that look to long-term economic development based on the tenets of sustainable ecotourism and avoid the temptation of building a tourism portfolio of cruise excursionists and large resort tourists that add little to economic development. In terms of ecotourism assets, Belize ranks very highly with a unique combination of Caribbean-style beaches, rainforests, biodiversity, and cultural sites based on its Mayan and Garifuna history.

Given the size of its economy, its physical attributes, and the government of Belize's current relationship with the cruise industry, Belize is the most likely country to consider ramping up their cruise excursionist portfolio. The struggle between the cruise industry and Belizean ecotourism will be one of the most important set of decisions for the future of tourism in Belize. Not only will the government of Belize need to set priorities for its tourism industry, but will have to do so as a very small economy, desperate for revenue, with a growing cruise industry very willing to send ever more excursionists to Belize. Since a lot of Belizean tourism occurs near the coasts and on the many cayes just off it, transportation around the country that also connects to the Caribbean is a major obstacle. While infrastructure is a major issue throughout the region, Belize should consider building infrastructure first around its ecotourism attractions so that they can better facilitate paying visitors who can help to finance infrastructure projects elsewhere.

Long before scholars thought and wrote about what is now called globalization, Panama was a global player based on its unique geography that let it serve as a major transit point for a variety of countries and cultures for most of its existence. While Panama appears to be less interested in developing a sustainable ecotourism industry than many others in the region, they have been very successful in attracting foreign direct investment and are well on their way to becoming a major regional player, if they are not already. Given the environmental impact of the Canal, there is a real danger that operation of the Canal will have a negative effect on attempts to build sustainable ecotourism—this is particularly acute since the Canal has long overwhelmed other parts of the economy. If Panama does not improve the environmental impact of the Canal, particularly after it is expanded, there is a real danger that the operation of the canal could very well preclude any kind of real development of sustainable ecotourism.

As small economies that were traditionally on the periphery of the world economy, there have been very few times in the histories of Nicaragua, Belize, and Panama that have held so much potential to change lives in each of these countries. With the consolidation of democracy and very little conflict since the conclusion of Central America's civil wars, now is the time for Nicaragua, Belize, and Panama to create a new future in which each country exploits its comparative advantage and opens itself to the world. Furthermore, as Costa Rica increasingly turns its back on traditional ecotourism and tourists that first visited Costa Rica now move on to bigger adventures, each of these countries has the opportunity to pick up a portion of Costa Rica's market share.

While there are a lot of positives lessons to be drawn from the example of Costa Rica, there are also aspects of the Costa Rican case that should serve as a cautionary tale for Nicaragua, Belize, and Panama. As this book illustrates, globalization and free market neoliberalism provide unique opportunities for small economies to emerge from decades of low growth, but that is not to say that the government plays no role whatsoever in economic development. Nicaragua, Belize, and Panama should take the positive parts of the Costa Rican model such as small-scale development and strategies to keep the income from sustainable ecotourism in-country, while minimizing policies that exacerbate economic leakage such as increasing cruise visitors.

LESSONS FROM NICARAGUA, BELIZE, AND PANAMA

Each of the cases presented in this book illustrate the need for a consistent plan of economic development that contain measures to make each country a logical destination for both tourists and foreign direct investment. Given the economic shocks that have often disrupted Latin American economies it is also important for each country to diversify its export portfolio to limit its exposure to downturns and to turn to nontraditional exports to minimize risks. Since cyclical downturns are more or less inevitable, it is also important for states to maintain a commitment to sustainable ecotourism and not change course when there is an economic slump. Part of the reason that states should stick with sustainable ecotourism despite an economic shock is the increasing evidence that tourism is at least somewhat recession-proof. This is based on a number of factors including the income level of international tourists and their self-perception as "responsible tourists" in addition creating a domestic tourism market can also serve as a bulwark for states against external economic problems.

Throughout much of their histories, states throughout Latin America have tried to construct an expanded economic portfolio that contains nontraditional exports because of the difficulties in relying on agricultural exports. As the case studies indicate, these attempts have historically been quite difficult. For states moving from a tourism industry centered on mass tourism, to one based on ecotourism and then finally to sustainable ecotourism it is very important that state policy encourage sustainable ecotourism that is nature-based, sustainable, educational and profitable. Each of these parameters is very important in order for Nicaragua, Belize, and Panama to succeed in sustainable ecotourism. While globalization holds a lot of positive potential for opening up tourists sites to the world, this same opening is available for every country in world. In addition, neoliberal policies will help to integrate countries into the world economy in a way that allows them to attract tourists as never before. Globalization, particularly the ability to research and travel to virtually every country in the world, will also mean that the expectations of ecotourists will be considerably higher than they have ever been. The extent to which these expectations are met will have a large influence on whether or sustainable ecotourism will be a successful economic development path.

While the idea of nature-based ecotourism activities is nothing new, it is important for the ecotourism industry to ensure that what they sell as "ecotourism" does more than just pay lip service to the basic tenets of sustainable ecotourism or an activity that simply occurs in nature. A big part of the controversy in the definition of ecotourism is the large collection of activities that have been categorized as ecotourism and one way to help determine what constitutes ecotourism is to make its definition part of the laws that manage government-based ecotourism development incentives. The best way however to ensure the long-term sustainability of ecotourism and to define exactly what it means is for states to utilize an ecotourism certification system that will help to discern what is or is not considered an ecotourism activity and also to quantify the extent to which ecotourism businesses are engaging in sustainable practices. While Costa Rica provides an excellent roadmap for a national ecotourism certification program, it could be very difficult for Nicaragua, Belize, and Panama to adopt the Costa Rica's schema or build one from the bottom up.

Rather than build their own ecotourism certification system, Nicaragua, Belize, and Panama could participate in international programs such as Green Globe, which certifies ecotourism businesses across a number of issue areas. Green Globe's criteria is similar to the Certificate of Sustainable Tourism in Costa Rica and assesses ecotourism businesses based on sustainable management, social and economic factors, cultural heritage, and the environment. Under its certification programs, Green Globe is already active in Belize and has certified a handful of ecotourism businesses. (Green Globe) Participation in a certification program would help to assure potential customers that an ecotourism business was engaged in sustainable practices that will help to ensure the longevity of the things that the ecotourist went there to see. It is particularly important that these third-party certification programs are rigorous and represent accepted industry standards.

The demand for ecotourism certification programs in Costa Rica emanated from the desire of ecotourism businesses to verify claims of sustainable practices from their competitors. While ecotourism certification schemes highlight the possibilities of supply-side, sustainable ecotourism, it is also important for ecotourists to play a role in sustainability by demanding that ecotourism businesses participate in certification programs. This sort of demand-side ecotourism certification could be a powerful tool for sustainability because of the power generated by the preferences of ecotourists and their consequent spending habits.

For demand-side certification to be successful and given the cost inherent in ecotourism certification to businesses, the key question is whether or not people are willing to spend a little bit more in order to preserve the environmental attractions they came to see and whether the cost to business is worthwhile. While the actual cost of Green Globe certification is not exorbitant—US$750 for a hotel of nineteen rooms or less (Green Globe)—there are a lot of contingent costs for businesses that need to make changes in order to fulfill certification requirements. In addition, these kinds of programs always come with a large labor costs for the business as inspections, paperwork and the certification process itself can be overwhelming. Although the CST in Costa Rica is fairly well known and utilized, the most common reason that hotel owners in Costa Rica cite for not participating in the programs is that they do not want to go through the time, effort, and cost of certification because they already do what the CST requires. It is of course also possible for ecotourism businesses to follow accepted standards of sustainable tourism even if they do not take part in a certification process. As Honey and Krantz (2012) point out:

> Even without a national "green" certification program, there are a number of national and international standards that can be used by the government and hotel developers and operators to ensure good environmental and social practices. Two of the most important are the Global Sustainable Tourism Criteria and the IDB's Sustainability Scorecard for Tourism Projects in Latin America and the Caribbean. (14)

Spending by ecotourists has a lot of power to create change and the evidence is building that most people who travel for ecotourism are concerned about their own environmental impact and the role of ecotourism in poverty alleviation. Recent surveys show that 96 percent of travelers think hotels should be responsible for protecting the environment, 74 percent think hotels should help to relieve poverty, 83 percent think they should hire locals, and 53 percent say they have a better travel experience when they learn as much as possible about the country's customs, geography, and culture. Most importantly, there is evidence that travelers are willing to pay more for these things as 73.5 percent stated they would pay US$3 a night for a hotel that helped to relieve poverty in the area, while 35 percent stated they would pay US$10 more per night. (Center for Responsible Travel) With the demand for sustainable tourism very high, there is a clear opening for ecotourists and ecotourism businesses to work together toward sustainable tourism and poverty alleviation in the host country.

One of the major challenges for economic development in Nicaragua, Belize, and Panama is to build an educational system that prepares students for the twenty-first century—both for skilled jobs in sustainable ecotourism as well as more highly skilled jobs in export industries. Although there is a lot of work to be done in states throughout Latin America, Nicaragua does a particularly poor job in this regard and will not reach its full potential if the government continues to spend among the lowest percentage of GDP on education in the Americas. The building of human capital via education is important not only for sustainable ecotourism to provide an educational element to what they offer, but it is also necessary to have an educated populace in order to receive more technology-based, and less low-skilled, foreign direct investment The need for human capital in sustainable ecotourism will allow businesses to hire more people from the local community who are much more likely to be motivated to encourage return visits from ecotourists because of their stake in the benefits of ecotourism. In addition, people from the community are more likely to be engaged in sustainable practices since they are a part of that community and are engaged in its future.

The need to involve all stakeholders in ecotourism management is a key component to being a viable, sustainable ecotourism industry. An important lesson for the building of human capital from Costa Rica is to create certifications and other educational opportunities specifically targeted to people who already work or would like to work in an ecotourism or hospitality-related business. In addition, given that the majority of tourists to Central America come from English-speaking countries, English-language instruction is an important part of ecotourism development. In Costa Rica, English-language instruction is so valued that schools start teaching it in the first grade.

As the Costa Rican case also illustrates, it is vitally important for policy makers to formulate policies that will help to create small businesses so that economic benefit can be spread across as much of society as possible. One of the first things to do is to improve the various areas in which the World Bank's Doing Business cites weaknesses. Since most of the measures in which states do poorly deal directly with slow-moving bureaucracies and issues related to the rule of law, states should engage in reform programs that make these processes easier for those who want to add to the economic life of the country. It is an interesting juxtaposition of issues when states make starting a business difficult while also trying to attract them by handing out large tax incentives for development.

Part of the reason that it is important for states to build a strong contingent of small businesses is that tourism has a very strong multiplier effect and these linkages help to improve the overall economy of the area surrounding the ecotourism site. The possibility of increased employment, spread around the community with as little economic leakage as possible, is one of the most promising aspects of sustainable ecotourism. Honey, Vargas, and Durham

(2010) argue that ecotourism has a lot of potential to create income for a variety of related businesses throughout the community:

> Tourism also has a vast potential for building linkages to other economic activities. It can, for instance, stimulate agricultural production, manufacturing, and services in the surrounding area. Visitor spending can indirectly generate more jobs, wages, and profits, as tourist expenditures flow around the economy. Another positive economic effect of tourism can be the diversification of sources of income for the family or the community. (76)

In addition, the multiplier effect has a particularly positive effect on the poor as they are not only able to diversify their incomes as they engage in small-scale ecotourism enterprises, but they also spread the income around to other small enterprises throughout the community.

> Although unreported for tax purposes, money returned to the local economy has a great multiplier effect, directly benefitting the poorest segments of society. In particular, the tourism industry fosters entrepreneurial opportunities for informal workers, from the sale of handicrafts to fruit vendors and others. (73)

One of the best ways for the poor to become a stakeholder in ecotourism is by the use of microfinance as way to help small entrepreneurs start a business by loaning them small amounts of start-up capital to get their business off the ground. Although microfinance has some drawbacks, it is particularly effective at assisting very small-scale businesses in areas associated with tourism. This could be craft sellers, food vendors, and independent tour guides. In Nicaragua, microfinance has helped many Nicaraguans to better their lives,

> In Nicaragua out of a total of 500,000 microfinance clients, the vast majority (are) located in urban markets, and the average loan is around $1000. When analyzing tourism areas like Masaya and Granada, the vast majority of the handicraft producers or small enterprises supplying foods and beverages to hotels and restaurants, do not have access to appropriate finance. (van der Sterren 2008, 41)

One of the drawbacks that need to be alleviated for microfinance to better assist small-scale ecotourism entrepreneurs is that oftentimes tourism income is seasonal, so level loan payments could be problematic for some individuals. In addition, Jos van der Sterren (2008) cites high interest rates as a drawback to microfinance for small entrepreneurs (40) and also found that the similarities among many microfinance loan products are not well-suited to the business cycles of the tourism industry because "tourism micro- and small enterprises depend on seasonal income and need to invest in fixed as well as current assets from the start. This irregular cash flow does not match the conditions that come with the standardized loan products (group loans, weekly repayments) offered by most MFIs." (42)

The development of sustainable ecotourism based on small-scale businesses will also help to limit the economic leakage inherent in many traditional sun-and-sand as well as cruise-based tourism models and will thus help to make it more profitable for the home country. The problem of economic leakage is nothing new for traditional tourism and despite the fact that international lending institutions pushed resort-style tourism throughout the 1970s and 1980s as an economic development strategy, economic leakage from large resorts became such a problem that "both the World Bank and the Inter-American Development Bank (IDB) were forced to close their tourism departments, largely because developing countries protested that foreign owned resort tourism had proved a poor development model because most of the profits 'leaked out' of the host country, typically leaving behind social and environmental problems and only low paying jobs." (Honey, Vargas, and Durham 2010, 16) Despite this, many governments in the developing world continue to use resources to attract large foreign-owned resorts via a wide set of government benefits.

One of the best ways for a small economy to develop an effective sustainable ecotourism industry that is nature based and local is for each location to develop its own set of comparative advantages. This is important because Nicaragua, Belize, and Panama, like any country have a unique set of comparative advantages that set them apart from other countries. As the case studies in this book make clear, each country has a unique set of characteristics that make it stand out. Due to this, sustainable ecotourism is an economic activity in which poor countries can easily compete with richer ones for tourist income. Not only are unique ecotourism sites a comparative advantage, but poor countries are better able to deliver an ecotourism product at a lower cost to ecotourists. In addition, Nicaragua, Belize, and Panama each have a clear comparative advantage in cultural tourism given their unique histories and cultures.

By developing their comparative advantages in these areas, Nicaragua, Belize, and Panama are well situated not only to compete with locations all over the world, but also to create become major ecotourism destinations in the Americas. With Costa Rica's movement away from ecotourism, there is a market niche available to states that can appeal to people interested in sustainable ecotourism. Each state's comparative advantage can also be utilized to create a domestic tourism market. This can not only serve as the backbone for an ecotourism industry targeted to foreign visitors, but also can generate revenue on its own. As the Costa Rican case illustrates, the construction of a domestic tourism market can be profitable in and of itself. A major part of the management responsibility for states needs to focus on strategies to limit the environment damage of an increased number of visitors. One of the fundamental issues in the management of sustainable ecotourism is how to both profit from and preserve the natural environment. It is necessary for tourism development to be managed for the long-term with a well-conceived and well-executed plan. Since the promotion of sustainable ecotourism is vital to its long-term survival, it is important for states to develop a strong government agency dedicated to development and promotion of tourism activities. The ICT in Costa Rica is a great example of a strong tourism management organization and it is particularly important that any agency have an adequate budget that allows for effective management of ecotourism resources. As Drumm (2008) points out:

> The failure of destination countries to budget adequately for tourism management in parks is eroding the very natural capital that visitors travel to see. If the current levels of investment continue, the tourism boom is likely to be followed before long by a bust. Prime habitats will become degraded, wildlife will become scarce, the quality of the visitor experience will decline, and eventually people will choose other destinations. (782)

The issues identified by Drumm are vital to the long-term viability of sustainable ecotourism and require a tourism management agency that has the power to regulate practices in and around ecotourism sites. While the ICT is a good example of an effective tourism agency, it is also important to point out that it is still capable of making short-term decisions that adversely affect ecotourism, particularly during times of crisis. It is also important to note that while the ICT was created in order to expand tourism activities as well as to protect Costa Rica's environment, the equivalent agencies in Nicaragua, Belize, and Panama were created mainly to produce revenue.

Since preserving the fragile nature of many ecotourism sites, one of the best ways to manage this fragility in places popular with ecotourists is to adopt a differential pricing system similar to what has been used in Costa Rica which will hopefully encourage tourists to visit less fragile parks by charging a smaller fee. Another indirect strategy is to educate visitors on the delicate nature of the flora and fauna and the need to stay on the trail and not touch anything. At some Costa Rican national parks the park staff has posted large photos of deceased wildlife that had been fed by tourists as an impetus not to feed the animals. An even better, and more direct way to manage fragile ecotourism sites, is to limit the amount of people allowed into the park. For instance, at Manuel Antonio Park in Costa Rica the number of visitors is limited to 600 at a time during the week and 800 at a time on the weekends. When the park hits capacity, the ticket-takers do not let anyone else enter until others leave the park.

The examination of Nicaragua, Belize, and Panama as well as Costa Rica also shows that policies designed to foster the development of sustainable ecotourism will also help to encourage foreign direct investment. This is vitally important given the difficulties these states have had in forming investment capital. As stated throughout this book, many of the same policies that encourage sustainable ecotourism will also encourage foreign direct investment. As the demand for sustainable ecotourism grows, this will increase investment into that sector. "A variety of market studies over the past ten years have documented strong and growing interest among consumers in tourism products and services that preserve the environment and respect local cultures. This growing consumer demand for sustainability, as well as the cost savings and risk reductions of sustainable development, is attracting the attention of international public and private investors and lenders." (Honey and Krantz 2012, 13)

As investment in tourism grows, it is important for policy makers to encourage investment and development in sustainable ecotourism and reject other types of tourism development that exploit the environment and provide little economic development in return. As such, the case studies in this book also illustrate the futility of using resort tourism, or even worse, cruise tourism rather than sustainable ecotourism for economic development, not to mention their impacts on the environment. In many ways, strategies to attract cruise passengers are the least effective ways to develop and prioritize tourism development. Cruise tourism tends to provide very little income for the cruise port, the cruise excursionists spend very little money in-country and they help to create an environment that is not accommodating for overnight tourists who actually spend more money on average. Cruise tourism is attractive to countries such as Costa Rica, Nicaragua, Belize, and Panama because of their desperation for investment capital and job creation based on their history of difficulties in attracting either. Due to this, far too many poor countries have taken what little they can get from the cruise industry and have invested heavily in it. Overall however, these investments prove to be a mixed bag since not only does a small amount of revenue generally go to the host country but "such investments will create jobs and income for host communities and countries. It will also generate pollution, increase congestion, and have other social and cultural impacts in port communities and beyond." (Seidl, Guiliano, and Pratt 2006, 222) Since there is some level of job creation and revenue in support of cruise excursions, states will often grasp onto whatever they can get.

The construction of large coastal resorts present many of the same problems as cruise tourism, except that since guests stay in-country longer and they will be more likely to spend more money in the local economy. In addition, resorts employ a much larger number of people from local communities thus improving the multiplier effect of tourism, even with a great amount of economic leakage. Given some of the issues with cruise and resort tourism that often work at cross-purposes with sustainable ecotourism, it is important for policy makers to carefully consider how they will structure their country's tourism business. Furthermore, despite the need for foreign direct investment, it is important to add businesses that provide the highest amount of economic development to the host country and do not degrade the environment.

PROSPECTS FOR THE FUTURE

Given the path of each country discussed in this book, it appears that Nicaragua and Belize are more eager to attract ecotourists and Panama is the most keen to attract foreign direct investment. Part of the reason behind these differences is that the Panama Canal is such an unusual economic attribute that it essentially subsumes every other development path in the country. Belize and Nicaragua on the other hand, have been much more interested in developing their tourism industries due to their very limited economic options beyond agro-export. While the potential of economic development based on sustainable ecotourism is clear, a lot of the success, particularly in poverty alleviation, is based on proper planning and structure of the ecotourism industry. As Klytchnikova and Dorosh (2013) point out:

> poverty benefits from the tourism sector are not automatic, and whether or not the poor receive a significant share of the benefits depends on the way the supply chains are structured and the way tourists spend their money. In order to ensure that tourism sector growth translates into benefits for the poor, complementary policy and investment measures may be required. (78)

Particularly important to the future of sustainable ecotourism are the complementary policy and investment measures that will make certain that growth is sustainable as well as disciplined policy makers who will not deviate from the plan. In addition, long-term sustainable ecotourism operates best at the intersection of open markets and sensible government policy. Neoliberalism and globalization have provided unprecedented opportunities for economic growth based on sustainable ecotourism and mitigating, to the best extent possible, ant economic leakage. While ecotourism, like any other economic enterprise can be cyclical, it tends to be less cyclical than other economic activities and has no "expiration date" on which ecotourists no longer find the country interesting.

Instead, what happens, is that states move away from sustainable ecotourism policies—mostly to either attempt to mitigate a short-tern downturn or to open tourism to new markets. One of the central ideas in this book is for states to develop a small-scale ecotourism industry that is both local as well as integrated into the global economy to take advantage of the mobility engendered by globalization.

Going forward, sustainable ecotourism provides a unique way for protection of the natural environment by a market-based approach. The increase in travelers coupled with the growth of environmental awareness has not only spawned an increase in nature-based travel, but has also made it possible for states to increase their revenue via environmental services connected to ecotourism. One of the ways in which scholars and policy makers have tried to assign a monetary value to environmental resources is through the idea of natural capital. Natural capital "refers to biophysical and geophysical processes and the results of these processes—fish in the sea, timber in the forests, oil in the ground—and the relationship of these to human needs over the long term." (Butcher 2006, 530)

The concept of natural capital seeks to provide a monetary valuation for environmental services in order to facilitate decision making on their use. One organization that has devised a method to measure the value of nature is the Natural Capital Project whose goal it is to "integrate the value nature provides to society into all major decisions. Our ultimate objective is to improve the well-being of all people and nature by motivating greater and more targeted natural capital investments." (Natural Capital Project) The reason it is important to provide some level of valuation for natural capital is that it helps to give the environment a voice since the monetary valuation of natural assets will pinpoint its value to the overall economy.

Another reason it is necessary to provide a valuation for natural capital is that

> despite their importance, ecosystem services are poorly understood, scarcely monitored, and, in many cases, undergoing rapid degradation and depletion. The Natural Capital Project uses science-based approaches and tools to account for spatial changes in these ecosystem services and their relationship to human well-being. We then use this information to inform decision making that leads to better outcomes for people and ecosystems. (Natural Capital Project)

In doing so, groups like The Natural Capital Project can help to give the natural environment a voice and better assess its impact on a country's economy and future.

In addition, assessing natural capital is beneficial because for many states "markets in environmental services are becoming the dominant approach to managing and protecting the environment." (Liverman 2004, 735) Part of what makes the idea of environmental services important to sustainable ecotourism is the exploitation of the environment via nonuse. The nonuse of resources for sustainable ecotourism will likely be a difficult thing for policy makers to embrace because it requires them to think long term and can cut off some small sources of revenue like cruise tourism. If, however, policy makers see the big picture and dedicate their countries to sustainable ecotourism it is possible to profit from the preservation of the environment. Due to this, it is necessary to devise a way to place a monetary value on natural assets. The valuation of natural capital in this way is one of the most difficult aspects of promoting sustainable ecotourism as an economic system of environmental nonuse, because devising a valuation scheme is not cut and dry. Making valuation even more difficult is that for some, the very concept of natural capital is problematic.

Another attempt to value natural capital is via a World Bank Partnership known as Wealth Accounting and the Valuation of Ecosystem Services (WAVES). WAVES tries "to promote sustainable development by ensuring that natural resources are mainstreamed in development planning and national economic accounts." (Wealth Accounting and the Valuation of Ecosystem Services) WAVES puts a valuation on natural capital so states better know the contribution of various environmental features to their economy so that they can be better managed sustainably. With ecotourism increasing rapidly, the knowing the valuation of ecotourism sites will be very important for situating it as an important economic resource and activity. Given the context of sustainable ecotourism and other more destructive economic pursuits, it is particularly helpful to understand the value of land and resources used for ecotourism and land used for agricultural development. In a study about ecotourism in Kenya, net earnings from tourism were found to be fifty times higher than from using the same land for agriculture. (Holden 2009, 22) With such a large difference between the value of resources for ecotourism versus agriculture, informing states of the value of their natural capital will help them to better understand how to manage these resources sustainably. The ability to arrive at a valuation for natural capital will assist states in building a successful ecotourism plan better focused on sustainable development. Despite many challenges for Nicaragua, Belize, and Panama, given the right plan, the future of each country is a lot brighter.

Bibliography

Agencia de Promoción de Inversiones y Exportaciones. (PROINVEX) proinvex.mici.gob.pa/, accessed November 16, 2015.

Alexander, Sara E. and Jennie Whitehouse. 2004. "Challenges for Balancing Conservation and Development through Ecotourism: Insights and Implications from Two Belizean Case Studies." In *Sustainable Tourism 2004*, eds. F. D. Pineda and C. A Brebbia. Southampton, UK: Wessex Institute of Technology Press, 129–42.

Andereck, Kathleen L. "Tourists' Perceptions of Environmentally Responsible Innovations at Tourism Businesses." *Journal of Sustainable Tourism 17* (2009): 489–99.

Arana, Mario. "General Economic Policy." in *Nicaragua without Illusions: Regime Transition and Structural Adjustment in the 1990s*, ed. Thomas W. Walker. Wilmington, DE: SR Books, 81–96.

Arias, Oscar Sanchez. "*Plan Escudo*." January 29, 2009. www.elfinancierocr.com/ef_archivo/2009/febrero/01/_MMedia/0000006821.pdf, accessed June 6, 2016.

Babb, Florence E. "Recycled Sandalistas: From Revolution to Resorts in the New Nicaragua." *American Anthropologist* 106 (2004): 541–55.

Bair, Diane. "Where to Go 2015." *Boston Globe*, December 27, 2014. www.bostonglobe.com/lifestyle/travel/2014/12/27/where/nzoddicYiMvnNerNoWvZyO/story.html, accessed December 7, 2015.

Belize Natural Energy. belizenaturalenergy.bz, accessed August 13, 2015.

Belize Tourism Board. www.travelbelize.org, accessed August 15, 2015.

———. "National Sustainable Masterplan for Belize 2030: Project Implementation Manual." 2011.

Belize Tourism Industry Association. "Belize Tourism Industry Association Stand Firmly against Major Cruise Port in Southern Belize and the Proposed Memorandum of Understanding between Norwegian Cruise Line and Government of Belize." www.btia.org, accessed November 14, 2015.

Bianchi, Raoul. "Tourism and the Globalisation of Fear: Analysing the Politics of Risk and (In)security in Global Travel." *Tourism and Hospitality Research 7* (2007): 64–74.

Björk, Peter. "Ecotourism from a Conceptual Perspective, an Extended Definition of a Unique Tourist Form." *International Journal of Tourism Research* 2 (2000): 189–202.

Bolland, O. Nigel. *Belize: A New Nation in Central America*. Boulder, CO: Westview Press, 1986.

Bramwell, Bill and Bernard Lane. "Editorial: Economic Cycles, times of change and sustainable tourism." *Journal of Sustainable Tourism* 17 (2009)" 1–4.

Brida, Juan Gabriel and Sandra Zapata. "Economic Impacts of Cruise Tourism: The Case of Costa Rica." *Anatolia: An International Journal of Tourism and Hospitality Research* 21 (2010): 322–38.
Burbach, Roger. "Et tu, Daniel? The Sandinista Revolution Betrayed." *NACLA Report on the Americas* 42 (2009): 33–43.
Burton, P. J. K. "Impact of the Pan-American Highway." *The Geographical Journal* 139 (1973): 49–50.
Butcher, Jim. "Natural Capital and the Advocacy of Ecotourism as Sustainable Development." *Journal of Sustainable Tourism* 14 (2006): 529–44.
Butler, R. W. "The Concept of a Tourist Area Cycle of Evolution: Implications for Management of Resources." *The Canadian Geographer* 24 (1980): 5–12.
Carse, Ashley. "Nature as Infrastructure: Making and Managing the Panama Canal Watershed." *Social Studies of Science* 42 (2012): 539–63.
Caumartin, Corinne. "'Depoliticisation' in the Reform of the Panamanian Security Apparatus." *Journal of Latin American Studies* 39 (2007): 107–32.
Center for Responsible Travel. "Responsible Travel: U.S. Trends & Statistics." www.responsibletravel.org/news/fact_sheets/fact_sheet_-_us_ecotourism.pdf, accessed December 16, 2015.
Central American Data. "Cruise Commission to be Created in Costa Rica." www.centralamericadata.com/en/article/home/Cruise_Commission_to_be_Created_in_Costa_Rica, accessed December 5, 2015.
Certificación para la Sostenibilidad Turística, (CST). www.turismo-sostenible.co.cr/en/, accessed September 25, 2014
Chase, Lisa C., David R. Lee, William D. Schulze, and Deborah J. Anderson. "Ecotourism Demand and Differential Pricing of National Park Access in Costa Rica." *Land Economics* 74 (1998): 466–82.
Choudhury, Birinchi and Chandan Giswami. "Tourism Revenue Leakage Check." *SCMS Journal of Indian Management* (2013): 67–77.
CIA World Factbook. "Belize." www.cia.gov/library/publications/the-world-factbook/geos/bh.html, accessed June 3, 2016.
———. "Nicaragua." www.cia.gov/library/publications/the-world-factbook/geos/nu.html, accessed June 3, 2016.
———. "Panama." www.cia.gov/library/publications/the-world-factbook/geos/pm.html, accessed October 17, 2014.
Cisneros-Montemayor, Andrés, F. Gordon Kirkwood, Sarah Harper, Dirk Zeller, and U. Rashid Sumaila. "Economic Use Value of the Belize Marine Ecosystem: Potential Risks and Benefits from Offshore Oil Exploration." *Natural Resources Forum* 37 (2013): 221–30.
Cohen, Benjamin J. "Monetary Union: The Political Dimension." In *The Dollarization Debate*, eds. Dominick Salvatore, James W. Dean, and Thomas D. Willett. Oxford: Oxford University Press, 2003.
Colón Free Zone, colonfreezone.com/, accessed August 31, 2015.
Condit, Richard. "Extracting Environmental Benefits from a New Canal in Nicaragua: Lessons from Panama." *PLOS Biology* 13 (2015): 1–7.
Cordero, Jose and Eva Paus. "Foreign Investment and Economic Development in Costa Rica: The Unrealized Potential." Working Group on Development and Environment in the Americas, Discussion Paper Number 13, 2008.
Coria, Jessica and Enrique Calfucura. "Ecotourism and the Development of Indigenous Communities: The Good, the Bad and the Ugly." *Ecological Economics 73* (2012): 47–55
Country Watch. "Belize 2015 Country Review." Houston: Country Watch Inc., 2015.
Croes, Robertico. "Assessing Tourism Development from Sen's Capability Approach." *Journal of Travel Research* 51 (2012) 542–52.
Croes, Robertico and Manuel Vanegas Sr. "Cointegration and Causality between Tourism and Poverty Reduction." *Journal of Travel Research* 47 (2008): 94–103.
Cruz, José Miguel. "Criminal Violence and Democratization in Central America: The Survival of the Violent State." *Latin American Politics and Society* 53 (2011): 1–33.

Culshaw, Fabiana. "*Las inversiones Venezolanas crecen in Panama*." *Debates IESA* 3 (2013): 75.

Cupples, Julie. "Wild Globalization: The Biopolitics of Climate Change and Global Capitalism on Nicaragua's Mosquito Coast." *Antipode* 44 (2012): 10–30.

Curry, Herbert F. "British Honduras: From Public Meeting to Crown Colony." *The Americas* 13 (1956): 31–42.

D'Amato, Anthony. "The Invasion of Panama was a Lawful Response to Tyranny." *The American Journal of International Law* 84 (1990): 516–24.

Destination British Columbia. "Cultural and Heritage Tourism Development." www.destinationbc.ca/getattachment/Programs/Guides-Workshops-and-Webinars/Guides/Tourism-Business-Essentials-Guides/TBE-Guide-Cultural-and-Heritage-Tourism-Jan2014.pdf.aspx, accessed May 26, 2016.

Diaz, David. "The Viability and Sustainability of International Tourism in Developing Countries." *Symposium on Tourism Services*. (2001): 1–18.

Dolnicar, Sara, Crouch, Geoffrey I. and Patrick Long. "Environment-Friendly Tourists: What So We Really Know About Them?" *Journal of Sustainable Tourism* 16 (2008): 197–210.

Drumm, Andy. "The Threshold of Sustainability for Protected Areas." *BioScience* 58 (2008): 782–83.

Dumroes, Manfred. "Conceptualising State-Controlled Resort islands for an Environmentally Friendly Development of Tourism: The Maldivian Experience." *Singapore Journal of Tropical Geography* 22 (2001): 122–37.

Duffy, Rosaleen. *A Trip Too Far: Ecotourism, Politics & Exploitation*. London: Earthscan, 2002.

———. "Neoliberalising Nature: Global Networks and Ecotourism Development in Madagascar." *Journal of Sustainable Tourism* 16 (2008): 327–44.

———. "Shadow Players: Ecotourism Development, Corruption and State Politics in Belize." *Third World Quarterly* 21 (2000) 549–65.

The Economist. "The Panama Canal: Now for the Next 100 years." *The Economist* 8900 (2014) 28–30.

Economic Commission for Latin America and the Caribbean (ECLAC). "Preliminary Overview of the Economies of Latin America and the Caribbean." United Nations Publications, 2008.

Epler Wood, Megan. "Ecotourism: Principles, Practices and Policies for Sustainability." United Nations Environmental Programme, 2002.

Everitt, John C. "The Growth and Development of Belize City." *Journal of Latin American Studies* 18 (1986): 75–111.

Feinberg, Richard. "Policy Issues: Competitiveness and Democracy." *Latin American Politics and Society* 50 (2008): 153–68.

Fennell, David and David Weaver. "The Ecotourium Concept and Tourism-Conservation Symbiosis." *Journal of Sustainable Tourism* 13 (2005): 373–90.

Field, Alan M. "Long Dependent on Services, Panama Hopes a New U.S. Trade Agreement Will Expand its Economy." *Journal of Commerce* 8 (2007) 14–15.

Financial Action Task Force (FATF). "Improving Global AML/CFT Compliance: On-going Process." October 23, 2015. www.fatf-gafi.org/countries/a-c/afghanistan/documents/fatf-compliance-october-2015.html#Panama, accessed November 22, 2015.

Financial Times. "Slow Latin America Growth Leads to Foreign Direct Investment Fall." May 12, 2015. www.ft.com/intl/cms/s/0/34d73822-f8b0-11e4-8e16-00144feab7de.html#axzz3sBCD65Kq, accessed November 20, 2015.

Fonseca, Pablo. "Nicaragua Constructs Enormous Canal, Blind to its Environmental Cost." *Scientific American*. www.scientificamerican.com/article/nicaragua-constructs-enormous-canal-blind-to-its-environmental-cost/, accessed May 27, 2016.

Font, Xavier. "Ecotourism Certification: Potential and Challenges." In *Ecotourism: Understanding a Complex Tourism Phenomenon*, edited by James Higham, 387–405. Amsterdam: Elsevier, 2007.

Forbes Travel Guide. "Why Nicaragua is Becoming a Travel Hotspot." blog.forbestravelguide.com/why-nicaragua-is-becoming-a-travel-hot-spot, accessed December 8, 2015.

Freitag, Tilman G. "Enclave Tourism Development for Whom the Benefits Roll? *Annals of Tourism Research* 21 (1994) 538–54.
Friedman, Milton. "Neo-Liberalism and its Prospects." *Farmand*, (1951) 89–93.
———. *Capitalism and Freedom*. Chicago: University of Chicago Press, 1962.
Galdon, Jose Luis, Fernando Garrigos, and Ignacio Gil-Pechuan. "Leakage, Entrepreneurship, and Satisfaction in Hospitality." *The Service Industries Journal* 33 (2013): 759–73.
Gallup-Díaz, Igancio. "A Legacy of Strife: Rebellious Slaves in Sixteenth-Century Panama." *Colonial Latin American Review* 19 (2010): 417–35.
Gamble, Andrew. *Hayek: The Iron Cage of Liberty*. Boulder, CO: Westview Press, 1996.
Gobierno Nacional, Republica de Panama. "Reseña histórica." www.atp.gob.pa/resena-historica, accessed June 25, 2015.
Gooren, Henri. "Ortega for President: The Religious Rebirth of Sandinismo in Nicaragua." *European Review of Latin American and Caribbean Studies* 89 (2010): 47–63.
Government of Belize, "Belize 2012: Economic and Financial Update, Ministry of Finance and Economic Development, 2012.
———. "Belize Sustainable Tourism Program." 2009. www.pcsdbelize.org/sustainable-tourism.pdf, accessed September 19, 2015.
Government of Panama. "Panama Government's Strategic Plan: 2010–2014." icee.usm.edu/panama-powerpoint-documents/Panama-2012/D.E.Sam_Leiva-Government%20Strategic%20Plan%20-%202010%20-%202014%20(2).pdf, accessed November 23, 2015.
———. "Panama Government's Strategic Plan: 2015–2019. cpublico.mef.gob.pa/images/stories/STRATEGIC_GOVERNMENT_PLAN_2015-2019.pdf, accessed November 23, 2015.
———. "Strategic Plan of Government 2015–2019: One Country." December 2014. cpublico.mef.gob.pa/images/stories/STRATEGIC_GOVERNMENT_PLAN_2015-2019.pdf, accessed November 15, 2015.
Graef, Dana J. "Negotiating Environmental Sovereignty in Costa Rica." *Development and Change 44*, (2013): 285–307.
Gray, Chris. "Responsibly Minded Will Keep Travelling." *Travel Trade Gazette, UK and Ireland* 2850 (2009): 7.
Green Globe. greenglobe.com/, accessed December 15, 2015.
Guillot, Craig. "Is the Nicaraguan Canal Viable?" *Planning* 80 (2014): 7.
Hames, Raymond. "Wildlife Conservation in Tribal Societies." In *Biodiversity: Culture, Conservation, and Ecodevelopment*. Eds. Oldfield, Margery L. and Janis B. Alcorn. Boulder: Westview Press, 1991
Hanson, Robert, Greg Warchol, and Linda Zupan. "Policing Paradise: Law and Disorder in Belize." *Police Practice and Research* 5 (2004): 241–57.
Harding, Robert C. *The History of Panama*. Westport, CT: Greenwood Press, 2006.
Harris, Sabrina. "Panama's Great Challenge: Reforming the Educational System. *Perspectives on Business and Economics* 25 (2007): 15–23.
Hartwich, Oliver Marc. "Neoliberalism: The Genesis of a Political Swearword." The Centre for Independent Studies, Occasional Paper 114, May 21, 2009.
Hausman, Ricardo and Bailey Klinger. "Growth Diagnostic: Belize." Prepared for the Inter-american Development Bank, Center for International Development: Harvard University, 2007.
Harvey, David. *A Brief History of Neoliberalism*. Oxford: Oxford University Press, 2005.
Healy, Paul F, John D. H. Lambert, J. T. Arnason, and Richard J. Hebda. "Caracol, Belize: Evidence of Ancient Maya Agricultural Terraces." *Journal of Field Archaeology* 10 (1983): 397–410
Heckadon Moreno, Stanley. "Impact of Development on the Panama Canal Environment." *Journal of Interamerican Studies and World Affairs* 35 (1993): 129–49.
Herman, Paula. "British Honduras: A Question of Viability." *World Affairs* 138 (1975): 60–68.
Hess, Michael, "Doorways to Development: Foreign Direct Investment Policies in Developing Countries" University of New Orleans Theses and Dissertations. Paper 680, 2008.

Hirst, Joel D. "A Guide to ALBA." www.americasquarterly.org/hirst/article, accessed November 24, 2015

Holden, Andrew. "Introduction to Tourism-Environment Relations." in *Ecotourism and Environmental Sustainability: Principles and Practice*. Eds. Jennifer Hill and Tim Gale. (London: Routledge, 2009). 17–30.

Honey, Martha. *Ecotourism and Sustainable Development: Who owns Paradise?* Second Edition. Washington, DC: Island Press, 2008.

Honey, Martha, and David Krantz. "Alternative Models and Best Practices for Sustainable Coastal Tourism: A Framework for Decision Makers in Mexico," Washington, DC: Center for Responsible Travel, 2012.

Honey, Martha, and Emma Stewart. "The Evolution of 'Green' Standards for Tourism." in *Ecotourism & Certification: Setting Standards in the Practice*, ed. Martha Honey. Washington, DC: Island Press, 33–71.

Honey, Martha, Erick Vargas, and William H. Durham. "Impact of Tourism Related Development on the Pacific Coast of Coast Rica: Summary Report." Washington, DC: Center for Responsible Travel, 2010.

Hornbeck, J. F. "The U.S.-Panama Free Trade Agreement." *Congressional Research Service Report for Congress 7–5700* (2012).

Horton, Lynn R. "Buying up Nature: Economic and Social Impacts of Costa Rica's Ecotourism Boom." *Latin American Perspectives 166* (2009): 93–107.

Hutt, David. *The Tico Times*. "Is Nicaragua's education system failing?" www.ticotimes.net/2013/02/01/is-nicaragua-s-education-system-failing, accessed December 10, 2015.

Huxley, Aldous. *Beyond the Mexique Bay: A Traveler's Journal*. London: Chatto & Windus, 1950.

Inter-American Development Bank. "Costa Rica to Improve its road and port infrastructure with IDB Support." www.iadb.org/en/news/news-releases/2013-11-20/costa-rica-road-and-port-improvement,10661.html, accessed December 7, 2015.

———. "Country Program Evaluation Panama: 2010–2014." publications.iadb.org/handle/11319/6971?locale-attribute=en, accessed November 20, 2015.

———. "Private Sector Assessment of Belize." competecaribbean.org/wp-content/uploads/2015/02/2014–Belize-Private-Sector-Assessment-Report.pdf, accessed November 1, 2015.

Instituto Costarricense de Turismo (ICT), "Tourism Statistical Yearly Report, 2011. www.visitcostarica.com/ict/pdf/anuario/Statistical_Yearly_Report_2011.pdf, accessed November 1, 2015.

———. "Tourism Statistical Yearly Report, 2013. www.visitcostarica.com/ict/pdf/anuario/Statistical_Yearly_Report_2013.pdf, accessed November 1, 2015.

Instituto Nicaragüense de Turismo (INTUR). www.intur.gob.ni/, accessed September 18, 2015.

The International Ecotourism Society. www.ecotourism.org/, accessed November 11, 2014.

International Monetary Fund. "Costa Rica 2014: Article IV Consultation—Staff Report; Press Release; Staff Statement and Statement by the Executive Director for Costa Rica. www.imf.org/external/pubs/ft/scr/2015/cr1529.pdf, Accessed December 5, 2015.

———. "Globalization: Threat or Opportunity?" 2000, www.imf.org/external/np/exr/ib/2000/041200to.htm#II, accessed August 3, 2015.

———. "IMF and World Bank Support US$4.5 Billion in Debt Service Relief for Nicaragua." www.imf.org/external/np/sec/pr/2004/pr0411.htm, accessed November 30, 2015.

———. "Panama: Growth to Remain Buoyant." www.imf.org/external/pubs/ft/survey/so/2013/car032713a.htm, accessed September 29, 2015.

Jackson, Ben "Freedom, the Common Good, and the Rule of Law: Lippman and Hayek on Economic Planning." *The Journal of the History of Ideas* 73 (2012): 47–68.

Jacobson, Susan K. and Rafael Robles. "Ecotourism, Sustainable Development, and Conservation Education: Development of a Tour Guide Training Program in Tortuguero, Costa Rica." *Environmental Management* 16 (1992): 701–13.

Jentleson, Bruce W. "The Reagan Administration and Coercive Diplomacy: Restraining More than Remaking Governments." *Political Science Quarterly* 106 (1991): 57–82.

Jones, Samantha, and Jennifer S. Lalley. "Assessing the Compatibility of Ecotourism and Hunting Through the Attitudes and Choices of Ecotourists." *African Journal for Physical, Health Education, Recreation and Dance Supplement* 2 (2013): 266–75.

Justiniani, Angélica Maytín. "Control of Judiciary Ensures Impunity for Panama's Elite." *Global Corruption Report* (2007): 252–55.

Kandil, Magda. "Spillover Effects of U.S. Business Cycles On Latin America and the Caribbean." *Journal of Economic Issues XVIII* (2009): 971–96.

Kilian, Lutz. "The Impact of the Shale Oil Revolution on U.S. Oil and Gasoline Prices" (December 5, 2014). CFS Working Paper No. 499.

Klytchnikova, Irina, and Paul Dorosh. "Tourism Sector in Panama: Regional Economic Impacts and the Potential to Benefit the Poor." *Natural Resources Forum* 37 (2013): 70–79.

Knippers Black, Jan, and Edmundo Flores. "Historical Setting." In *Panama: A Country Study*, edited by Louis R. Mortimer, 6–65. Washington, DC: United States Government, 1989.

Kraul, Chris. "Brazil Unfazed by U.S. Market Crisis." articles.latimes.com/2008/sep/22/world/fg-brazil22, accessed November 30, 2015.

Kroshus Medina, Laurie. "Ecotourism and Certification: Confronting the Principles and Pragmatics of Socially Responsible Tourism." *Journal of Sustainable Tourism* 12 (2005): 281–95.

Kwan, Pia, Eagles, Paul F. J., and Amber Gebhardt. "A Comparison of Ecolodge Patrons' Characteristics and Motivations Based on Price Levels: A Case Study of Belize." *Journal of Sustainable Tourism* 16 (2008): 698–718.

Lejárraga, Iza, and Peter Walkenhorst. "On Linkages and Leakages: Measuring Secondary Effects of Tourism." *Applied Economic Letters* 17 (2010): 417–21.

LePree, Joshua G. "Certifying Sustainability: The Efficacy of Costa Rica's Certification for Sustainable Tourism." *Florida Atlantic Comparative Studies Journal* 11 (2008–2009): 57–78.

Levitt, Theodore. "The Globalization of Markets." *Harvard Business Review* 61 (1983): 92–102.

Library of Congress Country Studies. "Nicaragua." lcweb2.loc.gov/cgi-bin/query/r?frd/cstdy:@field(DOCID+ni0013), accessed July 29, 2014.

Liverman, Diana. "Who Governs, at What Scale and at What Price? Geography, Environmental Governance, and the Commodification of Nature." *Annals of the Association of American Geographers* 94 (2004): 734–38.

Loáisiga López, Ludwin. "Daniel Ortega es más rico que Somoza." *La Prensa* (Nicaragua). February 7, 2009.

Lopez, Jaime. "Domestic Tourism Fuels Industry in Costa Rica." news.co.cr/domestic-tourism-fuels-industry-in-costa-rica/34461/, accessed December 8, 2015.

Lu, Jiaying, and Sanjay K. Nepal. "Sustainable Tourism Research: An Analysis of Papers Published in the *Journal of Sustainable Tourism*." *Journal of Sustainable Tourism* 17 (2009): 5–16.

Major, John. "F.D.R. and Panama." *The Historical Journal* 28 (1985): 357–77.

Manfredo, Fernando. "The Future of the Panama Canal." *Journal of Interamerican Studies and World Affairs* 35 (1993): 103–28.

Mária, Joseph F., and Daniel Arenas. "Societal Ethos and Economic Development Organizations in Nicaragua." *Journal of Business Ethics* 88 (2009): 231–44.

Marion, Jeffrey L., and Scott E. Reid. "Minimising Visitor Impacts to Protected Areas: The Efficacy of Low Impact Education Programmes." *Journal of Sustainable Tourism* 15 (2007): 5–27.

Mason, Carol Y., and Adagrace Rowlands. "Panama Canal Traffic." *Economic Geography* 14 (1938): 325–37.

Mattson, Sean, and Abraham Teran. "Education Trap Threatens Panama's Economic Boom." Reuters, www.reuters.com/article/2011/09/06/us-panama-education-idUSTRE7857D420110906#xOylXWekVS3qxqIY.97, accessed November 20, 2015.

McCullough, David. *The Path Between the Seas: The Creation of the Panama Canal 1870–1914*. New York: Simon and Schuster, 1977.

McPhaul, John. "Tourism Boom Threatens Costa Rica Eco-Paradise." Reuters. www.reuters.com/article/us-costarica-environment-idUSN1733128420080620#Fx844fDkL7pk5L6C.97, accessed December 5, 2015.

Méndez, J. Ignacio. "*Azul y Rojo*: Panama's Independence in 1840." *Hispanic American Historical Review* 60 (1980): 269–93.

Menon, P. K. "The Anglo-Guatemalan Territorial Dispute over the Colony of Belize (British Honduras)." *Latin American Studies* 11 (1979): 343–71.

Metzgen, Ydahlia. "30 Years Retrospect and Challenges Ahead" Central Bank of Belize. www.centralbank.org.bz/docs/rsh_4.5_conferences-working-papers/belize-30-years-retrospect-and-the-challenges-ahead.pdf?sfvrsn=4,2012, accessed November 6, 2015.

Meyer, Axel, and Jorge A. Huete-Pérez. "Nicaragua Canal Could Wreak Environmental Ruin." *Nature* 506 (2014): 287–89.

Midlarsky, Manus I., and Kenneth Roberts. "Class, State, and Revolution in Central America: Nicaragua and El Salvador Compared." *The Journal of Conflict Resolution* 29 (1985): 163–93.

Millett, Richard L. "Patria Libre." *Wilson Quarterly* 12 (1988): 98–103.

———. "Panama's Paradoxical Progress." *North-South: The Magazine of the Americas* 4 (1994): 21.

Moberg, Mark. "Continuity Under Colonial Rule: The *Alcalde* System and the Garifuna in Belize, 1858–1969." *Ethnohistory* 39 (1992): 1–19.

Montero, Alfred P. "Macroeconomic Deeds, Not Reform Words: The Determinants of Foreign Direct Investment in Latin America." *Latin American Research Review* 43 (2008): 55–83.

Moreno, Peter S. "Ecotourism Along the Meso-American Caribbean Reef: The Impacts of Foreign Investment." *Human Ecology* 33 (2005): 217–44.

Moreno-Villalaz, Juan Luis. "Lessons from the Monetary Exchange in Panama: A Dollar Economy with Financial Integration." *Cato Journal* 18 (1999): 421–39.

———. "Financial Integration and Dollarization: The Case of Panama." *Cato Journal* 25 (2005): 127–40.

Morgan, Murna, and Sydney Campbell. "Belize Tourism Industry." Research Department, Central Bank of Belize, 1992.

Mowforth, Martin, and Ian Munt. *Tourism and Sustainability: Development, Globalization, and New Tourism in the Third World 3rd Edition*, London: Routledge, 2009.

Mwakikagile, Godfrey. *British Honduras to Belize: Transformation of a Nation*. Dar es Salaam: New Africa Press, 2014.

Näslund-Hadley, Emma, Haydée Alonzo, and Dougal Martin. "Challenges and Opportunities in the Belize Education Sector." Education Division, Inter-American Development Bank, Technical Note No. IDB-TN-538, 2013.

Natural Capital Project. www.naturalcapitalproject.org/, accessed June 2, 2016.

Osborne, Alfred E. Jr. "On the Economic Cost to Panama of Negotiating a Peaceful Solution to the Panama Canal Question." *Journal of Interamerican Studies and World Affairs* 19 (1977): 509–21.

Padelford, Norman J. "Neutrality, Belligerency and the Panama Canal." *The American Journal of International Law* 35 (1941): 55–89.

Paige, Jeffery M. *Coffee and Power: Revolution and the Rise of Democracy in Central America*. Cambridge, MA: Harvard University Press, 1997.

Pereira, Juan Carlos. "FDI and CSR: The case of ProNicaragua." In *Responsible Enterprise, Foreign Direct Investment and Investment Promotion: Key Issues in Attracting Investment for Sustainable Development*, eds. Annie Dufey, Maryanne Grieg-Gran, and Halina Ward. London: International Institute for Environment and Development (IIED), (2008) 163–74.

Petch, Trevor. "Dependency, Land and Oranges in Belize." *Third World Quarterly* 8 (1986): 1002–19.

Pike, Joe. "Selling Central America." *Travel Agent* (2015): 10–11.

Powell, Robert B., and Sam H. Ham. "Can Ecotourism Interpretation Really Lead to Pro-Conservation Knowledge, Attitudes and Behaviour: Evidence from the Galapagos Islands." *Journal of Sustainable Tourism* 16 (2008): 467–89

ProNicaragua. www.pronicaragua.org/en, accessed November 30, 2015.

Puig, Martí I., and Claire Wright. "The Adaptation of the FSLN: Daniel Ortega's Leadership and Democracy in Nicaragua." *Latin American Politics and Society* 52 (2010): 79–106.

Ramos, Adele. "Belize and Guatemala Sign ICJ Protocol." *Amandala*, May 29, 2015. amandala.com.bz/news/belize-guatemala-sign-icj-protocol/, accessed October 22, 2015.

———. "Belize Missing Again from Corruption Index." *Amandala*, December 5, 2014. amandala.com.bz/news/belize-missing-corruption-index/, accessed November 3, 2015.

Randewich, Noel. "Intel Closes Costa Rica Operation, Cuts 1,500 Jobs." www.reuters.com/article/us-intel-costa-rica-idUSBREA371TJ20140409#SW5vewWVjyt1U6ct.97, accessed December 8, 2015.

República de Nicaragua. Ley de "Incentivos para la Industria Turística de la República de Nicaragua Publicada en La Gaceta," Diario Oficial, No. 117, del 21 de Junio de 1999.

———. "National Development Plan." siteresources.worldbank.org/INTPRS1/Resources/Nicarauga_PRSP-November2005.pdf.

de la Reza, Germán. "A plataforma formativa do Congresso do Panamá (1810–1826): A conjectura Pan-Americana revisitada." *Revista Brasileira de Política Internacional* 56 (2013): 5–21.

Ritchie, J. R. Brent, Amaya Molinar, Carlos Mario, and Douglas C. Frechtling. "Impacts of the World Recession and Economic Crisis on Tourism: North America." *Journal of Travel Research* 49 (2010): 5–15.

Rivera, Jorge. "Institutional Pressures and Voluntary Environmental Behavior in Developing Countries: Evidence from the Costa Rican Hotel Industry." *Society and Natural Resources* 17 (2004): 779–97.

Rogers, Tim. "Nicaragua is Unlikely Winner in Free Trade Pact with U.S." *Miami Herald*, April 9, 2011, www.mcclatchydc.com/news/nation-world/national/economy/article24621169.html.

Rowland, Ben, Durante Juan Jose, and Dougal Martin. "Belize: A Private Sector Assessment. Private Sector Development. Interamerican Development Bank, Discussion Paper #6, 2010.

Russell, Andrew, and Gillian Wallace. "Irresponsible Ecotourism." *Anthropology Today* 20 (2004): 1–2.

Schexnader, C. J. "Panama Owner and Contractors Agree to Final Cost, Schedule Terms." *ENR-Engineering News Record* 273 (2014): 1.

Schmidli, William Michael. "'The Most Sophisticated Intervention We Have Seen': The Carter Administration and the Nicaraguan Crisis, 1978–1979." *Diplomacy and Statecraft* 23 (2012): 66–86.

Schuler, Keith. "What Use is Monetary Sovereignty?" In *The Dollarization Debate*, eds. Dominick Salvatore, James W. Dean, and Thomas D. Willett. Oxford: Oxford University Press, 2003.

Seidl, Andy, Fiorella Guiliano, and Lawrence Pratt. "Cruise Tourism and Community Economic Development in Central America and the Caribbean: The Case of Costa Rica." *PASOS Revista de Turismo y Patronio Cultural* 4 (2006): 213–24.

Standard & Poor's. "Supplementary Analysis: Belize." Ratings Direct: December 11, 2013.

Silva, Eduardo. "Selling Sustainable Development and Shortchanging Social Ecology in Costa Rican Forest Policy." *Latin American* 45 (2003): 93–127.

Statistical Institute of Belize (SIB). www.sib.org.bz/, accessed August 13, 2015.

van der Sterren, Jos. "Financial Markets, Microfinance and Tourism in Developing Countries." *ARA Caribbean Journal of Tourism Research* 2 (2008): 35–43.

Steves, Rick. *Travel as a Political Act*. Berkeley, CA: Avalon Travel, 2015.

Stiglitz, Joseph. *Globalization and its Discontents*. New York: W. W. Norton, 2003.

Strassnig, Christian. "Rediscovering the *Camino Real* of Panama: Archaeology and Heritage Tourism Potentials." *Journal of Latin American Geography* 9 (2010): 159–68.

Street, James H. "Latin American Adjustments to the OPEC Crisis and the World Recession." *Social Science Quarterly* 59 (1978): 60–76.

Sullivan, Mark P. "Panama: Political and Economic Conditions and U.S. Relations." *Congressional Research Service Report for Congress 7–5700* (2012).

Sutherland, Anne. *The Making of Belize: Globalization in the Margins*. Westport, CT: Bergin & Harvey, 1998.

Taft-Morales, Maureen. "Nicaragua: The Election of Daniel Ortega and Issues in U.S. Relations." *CRS Report for Congress*, April 19, 2007.

Taylor, J. Edward, George A. Dyer, Micki Stewart, Antonio Yunez-Naude, and Sergio Ardila. "The Economics of Ecotourism: A Galapagos Island-Wide Perspective." *Economic Development and Social Change* 51 (2003): 977–97.

Theodossopoulos, Dimitrios. "With or Without Gringos: When Panamanians Talk about the United States and its Citizens." *Social Analysis* 54 (2010): 52–70.

Thomas, Kelly J. "A Model for Success in the Drug War." *FBI Law Enforcement Bulletin*, (2011): 1–5.

Thomson, P. A. B. *Belize: A Concise History*. Oxford: MacMillan Education, 2004.

Thurston, Daniel, Kayle Hackney, and David J. Boggs. "Discrepancies in Entrepreneurship Ratings: A Search for Answers in Costa Rica, Dominican Republic and Panama." *Journal of Management Policy and Practice* 14 (2013): 63–74.

Toledo Ecotourism Association (TEA). www.teabelize.org, accessed October 25, 2015.

Tollefson, Scott D. "The Economy." In *Panama: A Country Study*, edited by Louis R. Mortimer, 125–69, Washington, DC: United States Government, 1989.

Toth, Robert. 2002. "Exploring the Concepts Underlying Certification," in *Ecotourism & Certification: Setting Standards in the Practice*, ed. Martha Honey. Washington, DC: Island Press, 73–101.

Transparency International. www.transparency.org/, accessed September 22, 2015.

United Nations. "Proclamation of 2002 as the International Year of Ecotourism" Accessed October 19, 2015.

United Nations Educational, Scientific and Cultural Organization. (UNESCO) "Universal Declaration on Cultural Diversity." Cultural Diversity Series No. 1, 2001. unesdoc.unesco.org/images/0012/001271/127162e.pdf.

United Nations Environmental Programme (UNEP) "Tourism and Socio-Economic Conservation." www.unep.org/resourceefficiency/Business/SectoralActivities/Tourism/Factsand FiguresaboutTourism/ImpactsofTourism/Socio-CulturalImpacts/TourismandSocio-CulturalConservation/tabid/78782/Default.aspx, accessed May 23, 2016.

United States Department of State. "2014 Investment Climate Statement: Belize." www.state.gov/documents/organization/228796.pdf, accessed November 3, 2015.

———. "2015 Investment Climate Statement: Belize." www.state.gov/documents/organization/241693.pdf, accessed November 3, 2015.

———. "2015 Investment Climate Statement: Costa Rica." www.state.gov/documents/organization/241737.pdf, Accessed December 5, 2015.

———. "2015 Investment Climate Statement: Nicaragua." www.state.gov/documents/organization/241895.pdf, accessed November 24, 2015

———. "2015 Investment Climate Statement: Panama." www.state.gov/documents/organization/241908.pdf, accessed November 17, 2015.

United States Department of State Bureau of Diplomatic Security (OSAC). "Belize 2015 Crime and Safety Report." www.osac.gov/pages/ContentReportDetails.aspx?cid=17216, accessed September 26, 2015.

———. "Nicaragua 2015 Crime and Safety Report." www.osac.gov/pages/Content ReportDetails.aspx?cid=17797, accessed September 26, 2015.

———. "Panama 2015 Crime and Safety Report." www.osac.gov/pages/Content ReportDetails.aspx?cid=17190, accessed September 26, 2015.

U.S. Commercial Service. "Doing Business in Panama 2013." U.S. Department of Commerce, www.export.gov/panama/doingbusinessinpanama/marketoverview/index.asp, accessed October 29, 2014.

Usher, Lindsay E., and Deborah Kertstetter. "Residents' Perceptions of Quality of Life in a Surf Tourism Destination: A Case Study of Las Salinas, Nicaragua." *Progress in Development Studies* 14 (2014): 321–33.

Velázquez, Andres Felipe. "Panama: Cleaning House." *Latin Trade* 14 (2006): 50.

Vargas-Llosa, Alvaro. "Latin America and the World Recession." *Journal of Globalization, Competitiveness and Governability* 3 (2009): 20–30.

Vaughan, David. “Tourism and Biodiversity: A Convergence of Interests?” *International Affairs* 76 (2000): 283–97.
Vilas, Carlos M. “Revolutionary Attempts in Late Cold War Settings: Nicaragua in the 1980s.” *Journal of Third World Studies* 21 (2004): 45–61.
Walker, Thomas W. “Introduction: Historical Setting and Important Issues.” In *Nicaragua without Illusions: Regime Transition and Structural Adjustment in the 1990s*, ed. Thomas W. Walker. Wilmington, DE: SR Books, 2008, 1–19.
Walker, Thomas W., and Christine J. Wade. *Nicaragua: Living in the Shadow of the Eagle. Fifth Edition*. Boulder, CO: Westview Press, 2011.
Wall, David L. “Spatial Inequalities in Sandinista Nicaragua.” *Geographical Review* 83 (1993): 1–13.
Wealth Accounting and the Valuation of Ecosystem Services (WAVES). www.wavespartnership.org/en/, accessed December 15, 2015.
Weeks, John. “An Interpretation of the Central American Crisis.” *Latin American Research Review* 21 (1986): 31–53.
West, Paige, and James G. Carrier. “Ecotourism and Authenticity: Getting Away from it All?” *Current Anthropology* 45 (2004): 483–98.
Wickstrom, Stefanie. “The Politics of Development in Indigenous Panama.” *Latin American Perspectives* 131 (2003): 43–68.
Wilk, Richard R. “‘Real Belizean Food:’ Building Local Identity in the Transnational Caribbean.” *American Anthropologist* 101 (1999): 244–55.
Williamson, John. *Latin American Adjustment: How Much Has Happened?* Washington, DC: Institute for International Economics, 1990.
———. “Did the Washington Consensus Fail?” (Speech to The Center for Strategic & International Studies, November 6, 2002) piie.com/commentary/speeches-papers/did-washington-consensus-fail, accessed June 1, 2016.
World Bank. www.worldbank.org, accessed October 20, 2015.
———. “Doing Business.” www.doingbusiness.org/data/exploreeconomies/belize/.
———. “International Tourism, Number of Arrivals.” data.worldbank.org/indicator/ST.INT.ARVL?page=6, accessed October 31, 2015
———. “Logistics Performance Index. lpi.worldbank.org/international/global?sort=asc&order=LPI+Rank#datatable, accessed November 22, 2015
World Commission on Environment and Development. *Our Common Future*. Oxford: Oxford University Press, 1987.
World Economic Forum. “The Travel and Tourism Competitiveness Report 2015: Growing Through the Shocks.” www3.weforum.org/docs/TT15/WEF_Global_Travel&Tourism_Report_2015.pdf, accessed December 8, 2015.
World Tourism Organization (UNWTO). www2.unwto.org/, accessed August 28, 2014.
———. “International Tourism on Track to End 2014 with Record Numbers.” media.unwto.org/press-release/2014-12-18/international-tourism-track-end-2014-record-numbers, accessed September 22, 2015.
World Tourism Organization and International Labor Organization (UNWTO and ILO). *Economic Crisis, International Tourism Decline and Its Impact on the Poor*. Madrid: World Tourism Organization, 2013.
World Travel and Tourism Council (WTTC). “Travel & Tourism Economic Impact 2014: Panama. www.wttc.org//media/files/reports/economic%20impact%20research/country%20reports/panama2014.pdf, accessed September 12, 2015.
Yusof, Nor’ Aini, Ilias Said, and Faiz Abdul Rahman. “Sustainable Attributes in Lake Kenyir, Malaysia: Expectation and Experience of Ecotourists.” *The IUP Journal of Environmental Sciences* 5 (2011): 51–66.
Zimmerer, Karl S. “‘Conservation Booms’ With Agricultural Growth? Sustainability and Shifting Environmental Governance in Latin America, 1985–2008. (Mexico, Costa Rica, Brazil, Peru, Bolivia) *Latin American Research Review* 46 (2011): 82–114.
Zografos, Christos, and David Allcroft. “The Environmental Values of Potential Ecotourists: A Segmentation Study. *Journal of Sustainable Tourism* 15 (2007): 44–66.

Index

About the Author

Dr. Andrew P. Miller is an associate professor of political science at Wilkes University in Wilkes Barre, Pennsylvania. He teaches courses in comparative politics and international relations and specializes in the politics of Latin America, with a focus on development issues in Central America. His previous book, *Ecotourism Development in Costa Rica: The Search for Oro Verde* (2012) examines the role of ecotourism as a development strategy in Costa Rica. Dr. Miller received his BA from Illinois College, MA from Illinois State University, and PhD from Purdue University.

www.ingramcontent.com/pod-product-compliance
Ingram Content Group UK Ltd.
Pitfield, Milton Keynes, MK11 3LW, UK
UKHW041626031026
15587UKWH00001B/104

9 780739 180242